Intelligence and Intelligence Testing

Have you ever wondered what IQ is and how it is measured? Why is there such a premium placed on high IQ? What do we mean by intelligence? What does your IQ score mean?

There can be no denying the enduring appeal of IQ over the last century. It is probably one of the most misunderstood yet highly researched psychological constructs. Such has been the controversy surrounding this topic that it is difficult to distinguish fact from fiction. *Intelligence and Intelligence Testing* is a text that aims to address that.

This book examines the controversial psychological construct that is IQ, discussing and reviewing the history and current status of the research on intelligence and providing an overview of its development, measurement and use. From Galton, Spearman and Binet to the relatively recent controversy caused by the research of Herrnstein and Murray, this important book makes a major claim about the importance of 'problem-solving on demand' as one of the key components of today's notions of intelligence.

Chapters include coverage of:

- intelligence and schooling
- cultural differences in views of intelligence
- the history of IQ testing and its emergence into public consciousness
- IQ as a predictor of educational and occupational outcomes
- psychometrics and measurement of intelligence
- the future of intelligence research.

Written by Richard B. Fletcher and John Hattie, the author of the highly regarded *Visible Learning*, this textbook will be invaluable for all undergraduate and Master's level students studying the theory of intelligence and the impact

of testi█████████cation. Detailed and annotated further reading lists and a
█████████re also ████cluded.

Richard B. Fletcher is Senior Lecturer in the School of Psychology at Massey University, New Zealand.

John Hattie is Professor of Education at the University of Melbourne, Australia, and Director of the Visible Learning Research Lab.

Intelligence and Intelligence Testing

Richard B. Fletcher and John Hattie

Routledge
Taylor & Francis Group

LONDON AND NEW YORK

This first edition published 2011
by Routledge
2 Park Square, Milton Park, Abingdon, Oxon, OX14 4RN

Simultaneously published in the USA and Canada
by Routledge
270 Madison Avenue, New York, NY 10016

Routledge is an imprint of the Taylor & Francis Group, an informa business

© 2011 Richard B. Fletcher and John Hattie

Typeset in Bembo by
Pindar NZ, Auckland, New Zealand
Printed and bound in Great Britain by
TJ International Ltd, Padstow, Cornwall

British Library Cataloguing in Publication Data
A catalogue record for this book is available from the British Library

Library of Congress Cataloging-in-Publication Data
Hattie, John.
Intelligence and intelligence testing / by John Hattie and
Richard Fletcher. — 1st ed.
Provided by publisher.
    Includes bibliographical references and index.
  1. Intelligence levels.   2. Intelligence tests—History.
  I. Fletcher, Richard (Richard B.)   II. Title.
  BF431.H3487 2011
  153.9–dc22   2010035443

ISBN13: 978-0-415-60091-0 (hbk)
ISBN13: 978-0-415-60092-7 (pbk)
ISBN13: 978-0-203-83056-7 (ebk)

Contents

Illustrations

Figures

Tables

Preface

In 2003 and 2004, we were asked to be part of the two New Zealand versions of *Test the Nation* – a television programme that has been broadcast in many countries, it allows viewers to test their intelligence while watching a studio audience doing the same. Our involvement with these New Zealand versions involved us writing and reviewing many questions and tests to measure intelligence. One of the agreements we had with the television studio was that we could use our involvement to promote our discipline of educational psychology, and share in the use of the data generated in the programmes – the result of which is this book. Using a programme such as *Test the Nation* to unravel the mystique of IQ has been a fun and enlightening experience, and we hope our book will provide readers with a greater understanding of this complex concept. As well as describing how we approached the task of devising credible tests for a television programme that had to fulfill the dual criteria of education and entertainment, we also introduce the debates about what intelligence is; how, when and whether we should measure it; the controversies surrounding intelligence and many other interesting snippets about intelligence. We hope you enjoy this book.

1

What is intelligence?

If we said that we wanted to measure whether you can reason, think logi-cally, solve problems and use your memory successfully to accomplish these tasks, most people would agree that this is a worthwhile activity. Yet, if we said we wanted to measure 'intelligence', and particularly if we used the phrase 'IQ', it would be likely to provoke outcries such as 'You cannot measure IQ', 'You're a racist', 'IQ is a dirty word', 'There is not an agreed definition of what intelligence means', 'Intelligence is different across cultures' and other cries of woe. As a lecturer in psychology I (Richard) often say to students that there are three typical reactions people give when asked about IQ: those who like it (usually because they have scored or believe they will score highly on an IQ test), those who could not care less about it (they scored around the average score on an IQ test) and those who think they are a waste of time (yes, you guessed it – they scored low on the IQ test). What intrigues us as professional educators is the range of opinions that people proffer about intelligence and IQ and just how little of these are based on a solid understanding of these topics. It should be no surprise that the term 'intelligence' provokes such reactions, given the complexity of the concept and the many contrasting and often conflicting views people have expressed in regard to this psychological concept. This should be of no surprise given its often chequered history (more on this in Chapter 2). Indeed, its history has made some people wary of it and in particular the manner in which it has been used – sometimes with good cause.

The term IQ is often tossed about in casual conversation with little under-standing as to its meaning, its component or how it is measured – if asked, most people could hazard a guess as to what IQ stands for, but they would probably find it difficult to elaborate much more about IQ. It is the case that the psychological and statistical terminology used by the 'experts' often builds

1

smokescreens that can make research on the topic inaccessible and somewhat dry to the layperson. It is worth mentioning at this point that intelligence and IQ are subtly different, in that intelligence in its broadest sense is more related to the ability to acquire and apply knowledge, whereas IQ places this definition into a metric with the 'Q' denoting a quotient (something divided by something, i.e. IQ = 100 × (Mental Age/Chronological Age)). It is, perhaps, terms like 'mental age' that can be off-putting to the layperson as it is difficult to convey its meaning (even professional psychologists have difficulty with it). In many ways, the overuse of jargon and the smokescreens have been to the detriment of our profession; for our part we want to break open this very interesting but often abused concept so that you, the reader, can become more informed about the issues and current debates.

We have aimed to write the book in a style more accessible than the typical education or psychology book. We have provided references for more reading on the topics covered in this book in the Appendix, and those wishing to see defence for the claims we make in the chapters should seek out some of these references.

This book is essentially about intelligence and IQ. The 'I' relates to definitions and the 'Q' addresses issues of metrics, which implies the processes and issues surrounding its measurement. We do not forget the most critical aspects of IQ – that is, how we interpret the results as well as the conclusions we make about IQ. It is hoped that having read this book you will have a better understanding of what IQ is, how it is measured and what use it has or can have in today's highly technological and competitive society.

To set the context for more detailed discussion on the concept of intelligence and IQ, we begin by looking at everyday views held about intelligence. We then discuss differences in cultural views of intelligence, consider briefly the views expounded by the 'experts' and conclude with a summary of the major dimensions of 'intelligence' as perceived by 52 eminent researchers of intelligence.

The Ministry of Magic has always considered the education of young witches and wizards to be of vital importance. The rare gifts with which you were born may come to nothing if not nurtured and honed by careful instruction. The ancient skills unique to the wizarding community must be passed down the generations lest we lose them for ever. The treasure trove of magical knowledge amassed by our ancestors must be guarded, replenished and polished by those who have been called to the noble profession of teaching.

J. K. Rowling, *Harry Potter and the Order of the Phoenix*

Everyday views on intelligence

In a series of studies, American psychologist Robert Sternberg (1985a), then professor at Yale University, asked laypeople what intelligence meant to them. He found that people perceived intelligence as being related to reasoning logically, making connections between ideas and seeing all aspects of a problem. From this series of studies, Sternberg concluded that laypeople held one of three primary views of intelligence: problem-solving intelligence, verbal intelligence and social intelligence – all views that fit well with the attributes most 'experts' ascribe to the concept of intelligence, as discussed later in this chapter.

We also vary our beliefs about intelligence depending on the age of the person whose intelligence is being considered. For example, children are considered intelligent if they are good at problem-solving and reasoning; young adults, if they have high verbal and learning ability; and older people, if they have skill at social adaptation, usually about the more everyday problems in the world around them. Thus, we value problem-solving intelligence in children, verbal intelligence in young adults and social intelligence in adults.

The beliefs we hold about intelligence can make a big difference to our effectiveness. For example, Carol Dweck (1999) has shown many times that teachers who believe intelligence is something that is changeable and can be improved are far more successful at teaching than those who believe intelligence is something that is fixed and something you cannot change – regardless of the truth about whether intelligence is or is not changeable. In sum, the confidence that teachers have about their ability to change students' intelligence is a powerful tool for actually making a difference!

Intelligence and schooling

From a developmental perspective, primary/elementary school teachers consider intelligence to be more related to social attributes such as popularity, friendliness, respect for law and order and interest in the environment. High school teachers favour more verbal skills and energy, and university teachers see intelligence as related to reasoning, broad knowledge and the ability to deal maturely with problems. Thus, elementary teachers favour social intelligence; high school teachers favour verbal intelligence and university teachers favour problem-solving intelligence.

Having the positive attitude that we can change our level of performance can certainly make a difference. While some see such attitudes as related to intelligence (highly intelligent people are more confident of their success), there is much evidence that confidence of success occurs at all levels of intelligence – if you are confident you can improve then you are more likely to improve. Perhaps Norman Vincent Peale was right – we can build confidence to win and influence not only people but also our abilities. This is important, because intelligence, while valued as an asset, is not something that can be easily 'learned' via a training programme. It may be that a more important area for people to invest in is personal confidence. In other words, the question is not whether a person can attain a certain standing on a test or task but whether he or she has the confidence to tackle such tasks. As parents we would do better to believe that increasing our children's confidence to try certain tasks is more potent for enhancing qualities such as self-esteem and motivation than relying solely on outcomes such as IQ or achievement scores. The message is clear: We should seek to combine personal efficacy/confidence with the motivation to learn, which may relegate intelligence to a lower priority, and which should then promote learning for the sake of learning. By promoting intrinsic motivation and confidence to try new tasks rather than focus on intelligence scores per se, there may be more successful outcomes. It is most important that we teach children, particularly elementary school–aged children, that effort and intelligence are separate abilities as this will more likely result in 'effortful and confident learning', which in turn makes a major difference to their achievement. We will note below that many Asian parents emphasise 'effort' whereas Western parents attribute success in school and other tasks to natural ability, luck and good fortune!

It is likely that because intelligence involves reasoning and problem-solving there is also a skill in knowing when to use these various intelligence strategies. Certainly, if you do not have a high ability in these strategies then you are unlikely to use them, to know when to use them or to realise how critical it is to acquire them. There is a double whammy here: a person with lower intelligence may not have sufficient knowledge about how they solve problems (the jargon word is metacognition or self-regulation) or how to choose among various intellectual strategies and, most importantly, they may not comprehend the importance of effort and attention to the task – particularly when they encounter obstacles to learning. Fortunately, however, it is possible to teach

The test of a first-rate intelligence is the ability to hold two opposed ideas in mind at the same time and still retain the ability to function.

F. Scott Fitzgerald, first published in *Esquire*

people some of these strategies, and in particular to appreciate that effort, motivation and attention are important.

Cultural differences in views about intelligence

Just as laypeople in the Western world have different views of what intelligence is, so there are diverse perspectives of intelligence as we move across different cultures. The major difference across cultures relates to the importance of what we reason and problem-solve about. Some societies care more about problem-solving that leads to greater personal development (individualism), while others care more about problem-solving that leads to greater social harmony (collectivism) – and there are many variations in the balance of these factors.

Collectivism refers to societies (or people) that favour harmony, a sense of closeness and duty to family and others, seeking others' advice and a responsibility to the group. Individualism refers to societies that value uniqueness, personal independence, achievement, self-knowledge, clear communication and competition. You can imagine that what is seen as intelligence is likely to differ in these two types of societies.

Collectivists are more likely to see social intelligence, working with others, contemplative thinking, seeking the views of others, humility and an ability to know oneself and others as the hallmarks of intelligence.

Individualists are more likely to see verbal and knowledge-based notions of intelligence, speed of thinking, getting ahead and enjoying learning for self-improvement as the hallmarks of intelligence.

Collectivists consider rote learning and good memory as powerful tools for acquiring a deeper understanding of various topics. They see memory of facts as important for deeper thinking and intelligence. Collectivists would claim that we need to understand the surface features of things before we delve deeper into the relations between these facts or ideas, and particularly before we generalise or extend our thinking. In more individualistic societies, rote memory is something used often for quick success at passing exams or getting through difficult problem-solving exercises, but often this way of learning is not praised. Individualists largely view memory for facts as unimportant for intelligence. It is not surprising, then, that many Westerners condemn Eastern students as rote learners and fail to recognise that they are, indeed, using this technique to assist them in attaining a deeper level of understanding. This explanation of the different uses of memory in intelligence helps us unravel what John Biggs (1996) has called the 'apparent paradox of the Asian learner' – they come out at the top in the comparison of education systems across the world but we seem to not like the way they come out on top.

Another example of differences across cultures is silence. In some societies silence is a hallmark of intelligence, but that certainly is not the case in most Western or individualistic societies, where silence is often interpreted as the absence of intelligence. Similarly, some collectivist societies do not value the speed of thinking that many Western cultures do. Slow, contemplative thought rather than quick thinking is seen as the hallmark of intelligence in many non-Western cultures.

Another major difference across cultures relates to the purpose of intellectual thought. In many Western cultures, intelligence is considered a means for individuals to devise deeper understanding and to engage in meaningful debate. Many Eastern, particularly Confucian-based, countries see intelligence more as a way for members of that society to recognise contradictions and complexities, thus enabling them to more successfully play out their social roles and adapt to their environment.

Of course, statements about whole cultures need to take into account that there are many differences among individuals *within* those cultures. Certainly there are major differences within cultures about the role of social aspects of intelligence; an exciting concept that needs to be explored further. Within any culture, it should not be surprising that there are many different beliefs about what intelligence means. Some place higher value on social and practical notions of intelligence, some value verbal and nonverbal intelligences more highly and some place more value on cognitive and problem-solving notions. The common denominator is that intelligence requires thinking, problem-solving and successfully adapting to one's environment.

Experts' views of intelligence

The many 'experts' or academic researchers on the topic of intelligence come from diverse disciplines, ranging from education, psychology and sociology to medicine and politics. Not surprisingly, there are many contested views on what intelligence means. In 1921, E. L. Thorndike asked experts (mostly fellow academics) to define *intelligence*, and then again, in 1986, in another study by Robert Sternberg and Douglas Detterman, experts were asked how they defined

There is nobody so irritating as somebody with less intelligence and more sense than we have.
Don Herold

intelligence. At both times, experts indicated that they regarded intelligence in terms of adapting to the environment, using mental processes and higher-order thinking such as problem-solving and effective decision-making – quite similar to the lay views. Both groups argued about whether there were one or many notions of intelligence and about whether intelligence was narrow or broad in what it encompassed. The 1986 group included the ability to control or regulate knowledge, saw knowledge as more important and placed more emphasis than the 1921 definitions on the role of context, particularly the importance of culture in defining intelligence.

We discuss the history of views on intelligence and the development of IQ testing more fully in Chapter 2. For now, it is worth noting that the person who primarily set the foundations for our current 'expert' views on intelligence was English psychologist Charles Spearman, who introduced the notion of 'g' or general intelligence to explain a common attribute that seemed to underlie the many achievement tasks (Spearman, 1904; Jensen, 1998). However, although the existence of 'g' is largely agreed upon, the nature of 'g' remains hotly disputed. Others have claimed that intelligence consists of a number of primary cognitive abilities, such as verbal relations, numerical facility, memory and perceptual ability (Thurstone, 1938). Others have argued that there are various hierarchies of intelligence, such as fluid intelligence (involving reasoning, memory, inferences), crystallised intelligence (verbal, numerical abilities) and visual intelligence (picturing, mental rotation) (Cattell, 1971; Horn and Cattell, 1966; Gustafsson, 1984). Robert Sternberg has proposed three types of intelligence how people solve problems, how we adapt to our environments and how we use past experiences in solving problems and adapting to our environment (Sternberg, 1985b).

The one major exception to the notion that there may be only one underlying dimension ('g') is the claim by American psychologist Howard Gardner that there are multiple intelligences based on what people actually do, and each should be considered independently (Gardner, 1999). He has defined eight intelligences:

- *Linguistic* intelligence involves sensitivity to spoken and written language, the ability to learn languages and the capacity to use language to accomplish certain goals.
- *Logical-mathematical* intelligence relates to the capacity to analyse problems logically, carry out mathematical operations and investigate issues scientifically.
- *Musical* intelligence involves skill in the performance, composition and appreciation of musical patterns.
- *Bodily-kinesthetic* intelligence relates to the potential of using one's whole

body or parts of the body to solve problems.

- *Spatial* intelligence involves the potential to recognise and use patterns, images and pictures.
- *Interpersonal* intelligence is concerned with communicating and understanding others' feelings and motives.
- *Intrapersonal* intelligence entails the capacity to understand oneself, to appreciate one's feelings, fears and motivations.
- *Naturalist* intelligence involves recognising, categorising and drawing upon certain features of the environment, and an understanding of the role that culture has in our everyday living.

The claim about multiple intelligences, however, falters on a major issue: there is no evidence for the claim that differing intelligences are not correlated, and there may well be fewer underlying dimensions (e.g. working memory, verbal facility and even perhaps 'g'; see Akbari and Hosseini, 2008).

In sum, the major dimensions of most 'expert' models of intelligence include proficiency in abstract thinking, capacity to learn from experience and an ability to learn from and to adapt to one's environment, new situations and society. Perhaps the best explanation of intelligence is that in an editorial signed by 52 of the most eminent researchers of intelligence. Linda Gottfredson (1997) coordinated this statement, and it concluded:

> Intelligence is a very general mental capability that, among other things, involves the ability to reason, plan, solve problems, think abstractly, comprehend complex ideas, learn quickly, and learn from experience. It is not merely book learning, a narrow academic skill, or test-taking smarts. Rather, it reflects a broader and deeper capability for comprehending our surroundings – 'Catching on,' 'making sense' of things, or 'figuring out' what to do.
>
> Intelligence, so defined, can be measured, and intelligence tests measure it well. They are among the most accurate (in technical terms, reliable and valid) of all psychological tests and assessments. They do not measure creativity, character, personality, or other important differences among individuals, nor are they intended to.
>
> . . .
>
> IQ is strongly related, probably more than any other single measurable human trait, to many important education, occupational, economic, and

Intelligence is the wife, imagination is the mistress, memory is the servant.

Victor Hugo

social outcomes. Its relation to the welfare and performance of individuals is very strong in some arenas in life (education, military training), moderate but robust in others (social competence), and modest but consistent in others (law-abidingness). Whatever IQ measures, it is of great practical and social importance.

A high IQ is an advantage in life because virtually all activities require some reasoning and decision-making. . . . Of course, a high IQ no more guarantees success than a low IQ guarantees failure in life.

. . .

The practical advantages of having a higher IQ increases as life settings become more complex (novel, ambiguous, changing, unpredictable, or multi-faceted). For example, a high IQ is generally necessary to perform well in highly complex or fluid jobs (the professions, management), it is a consider-able advantage in moderately complex jobs (crafts, clerical and police work); but it provides less advantage in settings that require only routine decision making or simple problem solving (unskilled work) (pp. 13–14).

Overview of intelligence

It does appear that there is some intellectual functioning that is general across many ways of thinking. This general intelligence ('g') involves processing efficiency and capacity, it relates to the thinker's ability to stay focused on goals, and it involves the ability to uncover and deal with relations at different levels of complexity and abstraction. Such an understanding allows us to readily discriminate intelligence from creativity – as creativity involves creat-ing something new or different and the ability to bring together seemingly unrelated relationships between ideas or things. Intelligence is what we do when we do not know what to do.

There have been critics of this notion of 'g', who see our knowledge and reasoning processes as more modular or specific (e.g. having multiple intel-ligences). While the evidence for this latter view is limited at best, nonetheless we all know people with very high intelligence who are useless at various tasks. It is certainly worth knowing the areas we are good at, the ones we can readily improve, the ones we simply must admit our inabilities in, and come to value our other attributes that make us worthwhile in our own eyes and in the quest for good living and working with others. To discover these areas is a major use of intelligence testing – as it is often claimed to evaluate our proficiency in thinking to then undertake various tasks.

There is no need to agree to one single definition of a term (even dictionaries, the guardians of the history of words, include multiple meanings of most words). Any quest for a common and agreed definition is quite absurd.

Plato

Plato's (369 BC, Cornford, 1935: 99–100) notions of intelligence likened the mind to a block of wax, which could differ in hardness, moistness and purity. When the wax is pure and clear the mind will readily learn and retain information and not be confused. When the wax is muddy and impure then it will be hard for the mind to learn, locate and retain information. When the wax is hard the mind will be slow to learn and there will be no depth of thinking, and when it is soft it would be quick to learn but we can become confused as knowledge can be easily remoulded.

Einstein

In many ways IQ has become synonymous with people rather than with the actual concept itself. For example, mention the name Albert Einstein and the response will invariably include a reference to 'high IQ', 'very intelligent' or 'brilliant'. Einstein's immense contribution to understanding the physical laws of the universe is well known, even though he was not a university professor when he published his seminal 1905 paper – he was working as a patent clerk in Switzerland. But it is instructive to note that Einstein was not always viewed as one who would make a significant contribution to the world. One of Einstein's teachers admonished the future genius, saying 'Nothing will become of you' and 'Your presence in the class destroys the respect of the students'. Further, Einstein failed to get promoted from patent clerk third class to patent clerk second class in 1905 because he needed to wait 'until he ha[d] become fully familiar with mechanical engineering' (Bodanis, 2000: 5).

Having intelligence is not as important as knowing when to use it, just as having a hoe is not as important as knowing when to plant.

Chinese proverb

A physicist may struggle to *define* electricity or magnetism and would think it absurd and meaningless to try to do so. Rather, the physicist could tell you how electricity reacts with other attributes, how it can be used and the value of knowing some properties of electricity. By the end of this book you will have a better understanding of what we mean by intelligence and of some of the controversies surrounding the meaning, uses and misuses of this notion.

2

The brief and sometimes dirty history of intelligence and IQ tests

For many a scientific discipline it would be uncommon to claim that its history has been plain sailing and that its evolution has been uncontroversial. It is because science advances in a cannibalistic manner, devouring old theories for new theories, that anything that challenges the status quo is often met with disdain or disbelief and then the debate becomes embroiled in controversy. A combination of time and evidence, however, often results in new theories taking hold and, like the old ways before them, they become the accepted doctrine – until, that is, another challenger arrives on the scene.

Intelligence testing and its history are no exception and, like most branches of science, it has been built on the strengths and weaknesses of previous theory and research. Thus, the present-day notions of intelligence and its measurement stand on diverse theoretical foundations. We should be pleased that there is a diversity in views, as this makes for spirited debate and serves to advance our understanding of this often-misunderstood and controversial concept. Indeed, if the history of IQ and its measurement were not without controversy, this would make for a boring chapter. For the most part, we say the debate is healthy, and long may it continue.

As with most historical events, the social norms and ideologies of the day played a significant role in the development of intelligence and IQ testing. These concepts did not develop in a social vacuum and the developers, as well as their practices and outcomes, were very much bound up in the context of the times. We would be the first to admit that there *is* a tarnished history that sits behind IQ testing, but such a history is what it is – a history – and thus it should not be used to prejudge the current debates on definitions and measurement. Most people today operate in a world of political, social and cultural diversity, as well as equity, which was not the case in the not-too-distant history when IQ testing was emerging. Suffice to say times have changed, and we should be thankful for that; scientists today are more aware of the socio-political climate and are more constrained by the ethical, moral and consequential outcomes of their research. There certainly has been a tendency to 'politicize the debate on intelligence, or even regard certain issues (pertaining to it) as taboo' (Howe, 1997: 13). We were also well aware of these reactions throughout the development of the *Test the Nation: The New Zealand IQ Test* programmes, as were the Television New Zealand producers and staff. It is important not to be put off because IQ has been misused and abused in the past, but rather to look at where it is now and judge for oneself the merits or demerits of such a concept and also to take comfort in the fact that we have learned from the mistakes and successes of others.

At the centre of the historical debate on IQ and its testing are arguments such as intelligence is immutable and intelligence testing is merely a sorting device for placing people into neat, identifiable categories from which they cannot escape. Antagonists such as Stephen Jay Gould (1981) have argued that the perniciousness of the IQ testing process means that a single score does not take into account the complexity of the individual and context in which they exist. Above all, Gould argued that IQ tests are simply a tool to maintain the social order by confirming a person's societal position. After all, there are divisions in society and what better way to highlight these by using a seemingly 'objective' measure of ability. In other words, he argued IQ tests are blunt instruments with which to maintain societal order while at the same time allowing one to passively ignore the complex issues and problems that underlie differential levels of ability.

If only the debate were so simple. Sure, it is easy to debunk the whole notion of intelligence and the associated methods of assessing it. It is easy to claim that 'intelligence is what the intelligence test measures' but that because

There are three kinds of intelligence: one kind understands things for itself, the other appreciates what others can understand, the third understands neither for itself nor through others. This first kind is excellent, the second good, and the third kind useless.

Niccolò Machiavelli

measurement definitions are so narrow and culturally specific we should ban all intelligence testing. But such an argument is akin to throwing the baby out with the bath water. Most psychologists and psychometricians would agree that intelligence testing has its limitations, but most would also support the notion of intelligence as being a major dimension in an individual's overall psychological make-up and, therefore, something that should not be ignored (as Wittgenstein commented, 'The strength of the rope lies not in any one thread but in the overlapping of many fibres' – intelligence is but one thread). Indeed, measures of intelligence can be important in many ways, as Chapter 4 details. Yes, IQ has had some bad press, and yes, it has not always been used in the most ethical or defensible ways, but the same could be said about personality and many other forms of testing. In today's highly competitive workforce the preponderance of personality tests and their use when making important employment decisions about people is on the rise, yet there is too little criticism of these methods. This lack of critique could be because there have been fewer 'dirty' stories about the misuse of these methods, less connection in the past between personality and race issues and because the scientific community has been less rigorous in its attention to the measurement and use of these methods. So let us take a look at the history of this controversial concept of intelligence and its measurement – but please keep in mind our earlier comment that the history of IQ, like so many other controversial topics, is located within a much larger social debate that reflects the beliefs, biases and prejudices of the prevailing views of the time. While it is easy to ridicule IQ based on its history, it is harder to refute the notion of individual differences in ability, be they intellectual or physical, especially when one can see such variation in everyday things.

The earliest ability testing

From a historical perspective, ability testing can be traced back to ancient China in 2200 BC. For anyone wanting to work in the public office, the Chinese Emperor initiated a series of tests designed to find the most proficient candidates in areas such as law, agriculture, military affairs, finance and geography. The testing process was gruelling and often took many days to complete. The selection process began with preliminary examinations to identify the top 7 per cent, who then progressed to the district assessment. From here, between 1 per cent and 10 per cent moved to Peking for the final examinations, of which about 3 per cent would pass and become members of the Mandarin class of bureaucrats. The process was very much in the spirit of ranking individuals by merit and one can well imagine the stress and competitiveness of the candidates throughout the process. It was only as recently as 1906 that the exam was abolished. Such was the influence of the Chinese examination system that some European countries fashioned their civil service examinations in a similar manner and many continue it to this day.

Francis Galton

It was not until the nineteenth century, when the Industrial Revolution took hold and capitalism swung into full gear, that people began to show an interest in human capacity. Chiefly, it was the scientist Francis Galton (half-cousin of Charles Darwin) who began to develop methods for measuring many people's skills, and thus set his legacy as the doyen of measurement of individual differences. His incursions into the field of experimental psychology, as well as his immense contribution to statistics, marked Galton as a significant pioneer of the then developing area of psychological measurement.

Central to Galton's views on psychology was the influence of evolutionary theory. What intrigued him most was the notion of heredity – in particular, mental inheritance. In essence, he believed that reputation was a good measure of a person's mental ability and that genius was something passed on to the next generation. That is, prominent people tended to produce prominent children. The problem with his line of thinking was that it did not include the vitally important social factors affecting different groups. The son or daughter of a king and queen will one day be a king or queen, but to say this has anything to do with intelligence is hard to defend. While Galton's theory might suggest sons become as prominent as their fathers, this was, and perhaps still is (as in the case of George W. Bush), very much a function of social standing and privilege and not intelligence. Indeed, for many years (until the 1960s) some of the finest universities in the United States favoured admitting sons of alumni and aimed for graduates who would have the most influence on leadership in government and business – and thus had very small quotas on those who could enter on ability (Karabel, 2005).

There is no doubting Galton's influence on psychology and particularly his work on measuring individual differences. His main books, *Hereditary Genius* (1869), and *Inquiries into Human Faculty and its Development* (1907) were serious

Undernourished, intelligence becomes like the bloated belly of a starving child: swollen, filled with nothing the body can use.

Andrea Dworkin

academic works that aimed at shedding light on the mental inheritance and the improvement of races. These books laid the foundation of the eugenics movement, which was later taken up with great zeal by the intelligence testers in the United States at the beginning of the twentieth century. What the eugenics movement sought was to regulate marriage and family size according to hereditary parental capacity and (in Galton's case) this was defined as mental capacity. The argument was that if your parents were bright then you should be allowed to marry and produce offspring. The opposite was also the case and was, by and large, the controversial dimension – dull people should not be allowed to procreate and produce more dull kids. In developing a method for measuring mental ability, Galton mainly used sensory motor tasks such as reaction times. Hence, those with faster reaction times were by Galton's calculations the most intellectually adept. Galton's use of sensory motor tasks, along with the tests of the American James McKeen Cattell (who coined the term 'mental test' and whose work paralleled Galton's), was discredited as being too simplistic to capture the complexity of intellectual functioning and was, not surprisingly, abandoned, but their logic, as we will see, remained chillingly intact.

Charles Spearman

As noted in Chapter 1, Spearman was the person who was the most responsible for setting the foundations for our current views on intelligence. He noticed that when a series of ability tests were administered there was much overlap in the skills required to perform these tests. He introduced the notion of 'g' or general intelligence to explain the common attribute that seemed to underlie the many achievement tasks (Spearman, 1904; Jensen, 1998); 'g' has become a major, albeit controversial, psychological construct in the history of education and psychology. This has become one of the most replicated findings in psychology; while some may not wish to explain the overlap as 'g' or intelligence, some explanation for the commonality is needed. Regardless of whether one agrees or disagrees with his notions, it is extremely difficult to ignore Spearman's contributions to the field of intelligence and its measurement.

Alfred Binet

At the same time as Spearman was driving the theoretical debate, the French psychologist Alfred Binet, along with Théodore Simon, picked up the measurement baton where Galtonian science left off. Binet's approach to understanding intelligence, however, was radically different from that of Galton and Cattell, in that he believed individual differences in intelligence were much more complex than just assessing sensory acuity and response times. Binet argued that higher-order thinking processes, such as memory, attention and imagination, were most critical and that these were the key dimensions to measure.

The original motive for the intelligence scale that Binet and Simon developed in 1905 was to identify children within the Parisian school system who were not benefiting from regular forms of instruction. The implication was that intelligence was not fixed or necessarily due to any single cause, but that appropriate schooling could modify intelligence – this was in stark contrast to his predecessors. Binet's work, in effect, signalled the beginning of the special education programmes and the assessment of students most likely to benefit from these programmes (and those likely to receive benefit in the 'regular' or sometimes 'gifted' classrooms), which still exists in some form in modern-day schools. Binet and Simon's measure was aimed at assessing a child's general intellectual development and was composed of 30 tests, arranged in ascending order of difficulty. The tests ranged from vocabulary to physical performance tasks. It is important to understand that the motive for Binet and Simon in their testing of intelligence was not for comparative purposes but rather for identifying or classifying which children would be better educated in special classrooms.

The Binet–Simon scale was revised in 1908 to include the concept of mental level, which was simply the ordering of the test by the age level at which typically they were passed. So if 80 to 90 per cent of children aged five, say, passed certain questions then these were classified at the five-year-old level. So, for example, a nine-year-old child operating at a five-year-old mental age would be classified as being 'retarded' by four years and therefore a likely candidate for special education. The subsequent 1911 revision resulted in each age level having five tests as well as the age range being extended to adulthood.

The American adoption of IQ

It was, in many ways, the introduction of the concept 'mental age' that influenced much of the subsequent practices of the intelligence testing movement in the United States. Indeed, in 1912 the German psychologist William Stern,

It has yet to be proven that intelligence has any survival value.

Arthur C. Clarke

unhappy with the notion of mental age, suggested dividing the mental age by the actual age to get the 'mental quotient', which American psychologist Lewis Terman later multiplied by 100 to make it more understandable and thus called it the 'intelligence quotient' or 'IQ' (Terman's contribution is discussed in more detail later in the chapter).

The birth of this concept of IQ (as the psychometric measurement of 'intelligence') is a critical historical development that has shaped the debate regarding intellectual functioning and its associated uses. Once IQ had been defined and methods for measurement were established, it was then put to work in many different contexts. In general the argument ran along the lines of 'If you can measure IQ then you can rank people and if you can rank people then there is great utility in testing IQ'. Thus, as Stephen Jay Gould (1981) and others have suggested, began the mass-marketing of IQ, especially in the United States.

Henry Herbert Goddard

One of the first people to see the potential use of IQ testing was Henry Herbert Goddard, who translated the Binet–Simon scale for use in the United States. Goddard was hired by the Vineland Training School for Feeble-Minded Boys and Girls in New Jersey to understand more about the education and identification of categories of 'feeble-minded' students (today we call 'feeble-mindedness' developmental disability). Using his translated Binet–Simon scale, Goddard classified students using diagnostic criteria and mental age into categories he called idiots, imbeciles or feeble-minded persons.

Goddard's work soon found him sitting comfortably in the hereditarian camp, as his work reflected the same logic and sentiment as Galton's earlier work. What underpinned his work was the belief that intelligence was genetically derived and that 'feeble-mindedness' was the result of a single recessive gene. Later studies by Goddard provided data indicating that about 3 per cent of children could be classified as 'feeble-minded'. Goddard became concerned about the effects the 'feeble-minded' might have on society, and espoused views that children with such classifications should be segregated from society and even sterilised to prevent them from breeding. Such was the concern that 33 states in the United States of America passed laws permitting the sterilisation of 'feeble-minded' individuals, and more than 60,000 men and women housed in mental institutions were sterilised, with many not knowing what was happening to them.

Armed with his new hammer (mental testing), Goddard set out on a crusade to try to fix what he saw as a serious adjunct to 'feeble-mindedness' – notably, the influx of poorer southern and eastern European immigrants to the United States. What concerned Goddard most was their potential to compound the 'menace of feeble-mindedness' even more by their breeding with other 'feeble-minded' mates. Thus, the answer to this problem was simple: test all new immigrants arriving at Ellis Island and determine their 'mental' level and send back those with low scores. As we noted earlier, science often walks hand in hand with the dominant social ideology of the day; thus, Goddard's work at Ellis Island was, at that time, complementary to a view that immigration needed to be more tightly restricted and those with low scores on his test should be deported to their country of origin. What better way to justify such actions than by using the latest scientific tool!

The backbone of Goddard's operation at Ellis Island was a two-stage approach. First, an assistant would wander through the halls and visually identify people thought to be mentally defective (subjective bias as well as informed consent was yet to emerge as a debate in psychological enquiry). Once identified, the potential candidate, often confused and frightened, was taken to another location where the revised Binet–Simon scale, along with some other performance measures, was administered. If the person was found to be mentally defective they were often deported. How awful it must have been for those people denied entry to the 'land of opportunity' because they had the unfortunate opportunity to meet Henry H. Goddard and his troupe of testers.

Ethical issues aside, it is worth dwelling on the notion that Goddard translated the scale from French to English and then retranslated it into various other languages; therefore, the accuracy of these tests was likely compromised, given that French norms were used in the classification. Even today, translating a test into another language is a controversial and difficult process. This combined with the poor reliability and validity of the translated measures, as well as the huge cultural issues involved in testing people from such varied backgrounds and especially in these tense situations of border and customs checks, creates a grossly unfair testing process. The widespread use of Goddard's procedures at Ellis Island saw the numbers of immigrants deported grow exponentially.

Although Goddard initially held staunch hereditarian views, he later recanted his opinion in favour of the nurture over nature argument. In essence, he acknowledged that 'feeble-mindedness' was something that could be treated,

Love is the triumph of imagination over intelligence.

Henry Louis Mencken

and that institutionalising people on the basis of IQ scores was not necessary. One positive thing in Goddard's favour was that he helped draft one of the first state laws mandating that special provisions be made for special education classes. Obviously Goddard was a complex and contradictory man of his day (see Zenderland, 1998).

Lewis Terman

The next major event in the IQ testing movement came in 1916 when Lewis Terman revised the Binet–Simon scale and renamed it the Stanford–Binet scale (Terman was a professor at Stanford University and named his test after the university and in honour of Binet). Terman's contribution to IQ testing was enormous and the new Stanford–Binet scale set a benchmark by which all other tests came to be evaluated. Not only was the new scale increased in length but also it could be used with 'retarded' and normal children as well as normal and superior adults. One of the most radical aspects of the overhaul was setting the average IQ to 100 and the average variability around that score to 15 (see the normal distribution curve diagram, Figure 4.1, p. 45). The Stanford–Binet scale is in its fifth revision; its scaled scoring system has been adopted by many other IQ measures and it remains one of the more widely used.

One of Terman's lasting legacies was his use of the Stanford–Binet scale in his study of gifted children and their life trajectories. Originally started in 1922 and designed to run for 10 years, the study aimed to shed light on how 'intellectually gifted' children, if selected early enough and cultivated in the right manner, would eventually take their rightful place at the top of society. Such was Terman's interest in the intellectual development of these children that this continues to the present day. Of the 1,528 original recruits – 856 males and 672 females, nearly all white and living in California – some 200 (as of July 2000) 'Termites', as they are called, were still alive, some of them quite famous; for example, the famous educationalist Lee Cronbach and the physiologist Ancel Keys (he discovered the link between cholesterol and heart disease). Although the sampling of subjects was haphazard and subjective, some interesting facts have emerged. For example, more than two-thirds went on to higher education, 97 gained doctorates, 57 became medical doctors and 83 became lawyers.

The role of the United States Army

The First World War provided the catalyst for the development and mass use of IQ tests. Both Goddard's and Terman's influence on IQ testing meant that they were often invited to work with some of the most prominent psychologists of the day. As a member of Robert Yerkes' testing team at Yale University, Goddard was involved in the development and administration of the United States Army Alpha and Beta tests, which differed markedly from earlier IQ tests. Whereas the Binet–Simon scale, and its translated versions, was individually administered, the army Alpha and Beta tests were developed for group testing. The advantage of this approach was that recruits could be tested and scored quicker. Thus, IQ testing developed into an efficient, scientifically-based industry, which over the years has grown in importance (examples include the Educational Testing Service and the Law School Admission Test). IQ testing had truly come of age.

The Alpha and Beta tests were administered to identify those recruits with low intelligence as well as those suited to certain jobs or officer training. The Alpha test was used with recruits who could read and write, whereas the Beta test was used for illiterate recruits or those who could not speak English. Like most of the early IQ tests, little was known about their psychometric properties. For example, the Beta test was usually administered to large groups by the examiner, who used pictorial cues as well as hand signals and facial expressions when reading each question aloud. One of the main criticisms of the Army Alpha and Beta tests was the lack of uniformity of the conditions for giving the test, as well as the variability of the examiners, both of which can dramatically affect the validity of the scores. Although the tests were given to more than 1.75 million soldiers, it is unclear whether the testing programme made any difference to military functioning or efficiency. Indeed, many higher-ranking military officers were sceptical about the uses of psychological testing and, thus, much of the data went unused. After the war, it was found that while the Alpha test had high reliability, it had lower validity for predicting 'officer material' – indeed, the Alpha tests were better predictors of truck driving, which would surprise few who have watched movie footage of the US troops in battle. (Reliability and validity are important attributes of measurement and are discussed more fully in Chapter 4.)

One person who did use the army Alpha tests was Carl Brigham, who in 1923 analysed the racial differences between recruits. He concluded that African Americans and Mediterranean and Alpine recruits were 'intellectually inferior',

Anyone who conducts an argument by appealing to authority is not using his intelligence; he is just using his memory.

Leonardo da Vinci

and so continued the many debates on IQ and ethnicity. Like his colleague Goddard, Brigham later recanted and attributed these differences to language and cultural differences.

Sir Cyril Burt

With the rise of Nazism and its beliefs about racial superiority, it is not surprising that the eugenics movement lost favour and momentum in the West. That is not to say that IQ disappeared from view; it merely meant that other means of showing the link between IQ and hereditary needed to be found, and thus entered the first knight of psychology: Sir Cyril Burt. There is no denying Cyril Burt's influence on psychology, especially his development of educational psychology. He was also instrumental in refining the statistical technique of factor analysis, which is still at the forefront of most psychological research today. Factor analysis is a complex correlational technique that is used to detect if groups of questions or tests share a common underlying theme. It is the critical method used in determining if measures can be compartmentalised into smaller units. Thus, it can test if overall IQ has subdimensions, such as numerical reasoning, verbal analogy and so on, and whether these subdimensions can be meaningfully weighted to form a single (unidimensional) score.

Cyril Burt was a staunch hereditarian who undertook his pioneering work on special education in Britain throughout the twentieth century, and has been (falsely) attributed as the father of the eleven-plus examination, whereby children sit tests at age 11 to decide on the nature of the high school they attend (academic, vocational and so on). Indeed, Burt argued that IQ tests, like the 11-plus examination, could be used to identify children from the lower classes who could profit from a more academic schooling (he was certain that intelligence genes were not confined to the British upper class). He also started the largest study of identical twins who had been separated at birth and reared in different families.

Burt, like many researchers in the area of intelligence, was subjected to many personal barbs and the greatest was the accusation of fraud, published after he died in 1976. A front-page news item in a British newspaper claimed that Burt was a fraud because he invented crucial data. His biographer, Hearnshaw (1979), also made various claims against Burt: he could not have possibly collected some of his post-war data and thus he fabricated them by inventing data to fit his theories; his work was an 'elaborately constructed piece of work' based on invented data; some of his co-workers were fictitious; he used his position to change other researchers' papers to reflect better his views and contributions; and he altered the history of his area to claim priority over some contributors.

> He falsified history in the interest of self-aggrandizement. That he was guilty of malfeasance there can be no reasonable doubt. The only question at issue can be, was he guilty simpliciter or guilty with diminished responsibility as a result of pathological influences?

> (p. 180)

Hearnshaw answered the question by supporting the latter argument.

The reason why Burt undertook these actions was, claimed his biographer, because he had Ménière's disease, which is typical of obsessive–compulsive types – the connection is abject nonsense. During his childhood, claimed Hearnshaw, he was forced to survive by observing his peers and enemies closely, 'to keep his feelings to himself, to bluff it out, and to outmanoeuvre those who tried to molest him' (Hearnshaw, 1979: 273). Hearnshaw's claim is that Burt learned his deviousness because he studied Greek and Latin for ten years as a student – as, in preparation of producing pieces of Greek and Latin prose, the perfect copy or fake achieves the highest mark – hence he was trained in copying and faking! 'In the lost boyhood of Cyril Burt psychology was betrayed'. Worse, in his adulthood he was not a 'sociable or clubbable man' (p. 291).

None of these accusations have withstood critique – although Burt may have been careless and not always clear in his methods – but his reputation has been sullied. His work, however, has been replicated so many times that it almost does not matter whether he was a fraud or not (Joynson, 1989; Hattie, 1991). But the claims are not uncommon for researchers studying this topic; there are many critics. Recently, as another example, a noted American scholar, Linda Gottfredson, has spoken about the accusations, deceit and harassment she has experienced because of her work on intelligence (Wainer and Robinson, 2009). The most famous case of death threats, rioting and ugly critique relates to Arthur Jensen (see next section). Since the 1970s, intelligence and IQ testing has lost its aura of mainstream respectability: in many places IQ tests have been banned, research on the topic has diminished, new names are being invented to test developers and users do not have to use 'IQ' for things such as problem-

Great spirits have always found violent opposition from mediocrities. The latter cannot understand it when a man does not thoughtlessly submit to hereditary prejudices but honestly and courageously uses his intelligence.

Albert Einstein

solving and differential abilities. One of the now more popular IQ measures is called the 'assessment battery for children.'

Arthur R. Jensen

In 1969, Arthur R. Jensen, a Berkeley psychologist, published a controversial paper in the *Harvard Educational Review*. In his paper, Jensen approached the now taboo subject of race and IQ by highlighting the interplay between nature (genetics) and nurture (environment) in explaining differences between African Americans and Caucasians. Jensen's paper was primarily an attack on the utility of compensatory education – that is, education designed to lessen the gap in achievement between those from minority backgrounds compared with those from the majority. In particular, Jensen argued that environment alone was not the sole cause for any disparity between certain groups, and factors such as genetics may explain some of the achievement score differences, thus compensatory education was not the means to close the gap. But it was one sentence that caused an uproar: 'The preponderance of the evidence is, in my opinion, less consistent with a strictly environmental hypothesis than with a genetic hypothesis, which, of course, does not exclude the influence of environment or its interaction with genetic factors' (p. 82). This claim that there may be innate differences between blacks and whites on IQ prompted a torrent of abuse, and Jensen was heckled, threatened, abused and generally vilified. Jensen went on to become one of the most eminent scholars in the field of intelligence and continued his research on the differences between the IQ of various groups, although this is not as well known. It is not the fact that there are differences in IQ scores across groups that is contentious; it is the claimed reasons for this difference.

The Flynn effect

We also know, thanks to New Zealand scholar James Flynn, that there has been an increase in the average IQ over the generations. For example, it is now well documented that *both* African–American and Caucasians gained 15 IQ points during the past 30 years. So in one sense, the African–American community has closed the entire 'gap', which certainly demonstrates the power of environment (the problem is that the Caucasian IQ has also increased 12 to 15 IQ points during this same period).

Indeed, this effect, now called the 'Flynn effect', is well established. Nations, almost without exception, have shown gains of about 20 IQ points per generation (30 years). These gains are highest for IQ tests that are most related to reasoning and the capacity to figure out novel problems (this is often called 'fluid intelligence', see Chapter 5); and least related to knowledge, which arises from better educational opportunity, a history of persistence and good motivation for learning (this is often called 'crystallised intelligence', see Chapter 5). It is, therefore, important to note that these gains in IQ across decades and generations is *not* related to the type of knowledge gained from increased schooling, increased test-taking sophistication, increased nutrition, greater urbanisation, eradication of childhood diseases, upgrading of early childhood or preschool programmes or education in general.

Herrnstein and Murray

Perhaps the best instance of extreme argument about IQ and race differences is Richard Herrnstein and Charles Murray's now-infamous 1994 book *The Bell Curve*. The book includes reports of many research studies, but it was the authors' interpretations of the research that caused an outcry. For example, when citing research on the relation between IQ and illegitimacy, they noted that

> the smarter a woman is, the more likely that she deliberately decides to have a child and calculates the best time to do it. The less intelligent the woman is, the more likely that she does not think ahead from sex to procreation, does not remember to use birth control, does not carefully consider when and under what circumstances she should have a child. How intelligent a woman is may interact with her impulsiveness, and hence her ability to exert self-discipline and restraint on her partner in order to avoid pregnancy.
>
> (p. 179)

They go on to conclude that 'low intelligence is an important independent cause of illegitimacy' (p. 189). Such (il)logic and the assumption that having a baby is entirely up to one sex, the omission of mentioning the father, and the conclusion of 'welfare being the prime suspect' is more rhetoric than research.

Military intelligence is a contradiction in terms.

Groucho Marx

They also used other studies on intelligence to stretch claims so that they could make particular public policy statements. For example, Herrnstein and Murray argued that the United States is run by rules congenial to people with high IQs and that makes life more difficult for everyone else. Herrnstein and Murray argue that this has led to the creation of complicated, sophisticated systems of fairness, justice and right and wrong that those creating such systems claim are ethically superior to simple, black-and-white versions. Hence the recommendation from Herrnstein and Murray to have less government, let business be business – unhampered by complicated rules – let communities make their own decisions, have less welfare and centralised handouts, and so forth.

The Bell Curve was a reawakening of the Jensen debates, although it did not last as long as or have the same depth of scholarly analysis associated with Jensen's works. There were reactions in newspapers and popular journals, books attacking the claims and spurious logic, but the overwhelming reaction was 'Sigh, here we go again'. Both the more outlandish claims and scholarly debate is likely to continue on the topic of IQ differences between race and cultural groups, and we could be optimistic if we could discover ways to reduce these gaps.

IQ research today

The debates about IQ today are rarely mainstream for psychologists. Instead, research is more related to the notions of 'cognitive functioning', developed during the 1970s and 1980s, whereby there is a search for the various strategies and manners in which we process information. This has led to the identification of many strategies, and some researchers seem to be concerned that some of us have more versatility and expertise in the use of these strategies and that this seems to relate to the notion of general intelligence, or 'g'. In many ways, researchers of today rarely refer to the notion of 'g'. This makes life easier as it avoids the debates about race, heredity and 'designer genes'; but one does not need to scratch too far beyond the surface to note that the issues of IQ are still present.

Neither a lofty degree of intelligence nor imagination nor both together go to the making of genius. Love, love, love, that is the soul of genius.

Wolfgang Amadeus Mozart

The small number of researchers who are still publishing on intelligence today are more focused on the nature of 'g' and the many dimensions of intelligence. It seems that older rejected theories (such as faculty psychology, which assumed that there were various bumps on the head that could be traced to different thinking patterns) have been reinvented in the name of multiple intelligences and dimension theories of intelligence – that is, there is a denial of the notion of 'g' and a denial that whenever tests of cognitive abilities are related to each other there is a source of commonality that can explain these relations. These newer 'g'-denial theories have not influenced the work of psychologists very much (as these theories have limited support for them), but they are sufficiently seductive to be very evident and are present in some educational claims.

There is a large amount of research seeking alternative measures of 'g' using brain functioning, blood flow and other physiological cues. This may be fascinating but is unlikely to lead to much change in the debate if the major impact is to replace IQ tests with neurological-based measures. We may have a semblance of more pure, or cultural-free, measures, but any new physiologically based test will still only be as important as its capacity to predict and explain our thinking – and we have already rehearsed these debates over the past century with psychologically based tests.

The concept of IQ has an enduring appeal, although for the past 40 years its popularity has been waning. Despite this waxing and waning, IQ has emerged in many different forms and has found its rank among the plethora of theoretically and empirically based psychological constructs. Indeed, it stands out as being one of the most well-supported notions in educational and mainstream psychology, with many uses in education, industry and health, to name but a few.

Researchers and practitioners most certainly have learned from the mistakes and abuses of the past, and contemporary IQ tests reflect the advances made in test construction, scoring and analysis (more on this in Chapter 5). Although the criticisms of IQ from people such as Stephen Jay Gould (1981), the accusations of fraud about Burt and the tensions raised concerning Jensen's research have not benefited the reputation of IQ, there is much that is good in the modern research literature; for example, the use of IQ tests in identifying patients with Alzheimer's or Parkinson's disease, identification of children who have not had opportunities to learn but have remarkable cognitive thinking skills, and ensuring that students with some physical disadvantages are not then considered to

Truly great madness cannot be achieved without significant intelligence.

Henrik Tikkanen

be unable to think and not derive benefit from schooling – to name a few. The next chapter looks more closely at some of the benefits of research relating to intelligence and IQ measures.

As with many research areas where controversy abounds, this provides a healthy forum to check the positives and negatives of each argument. This, indeed, is the manner in which science advances. The net result is that the theory with the most evidence will likely gain the foreground (or the one without damning evidence against it) and must then be prepared to take on new challengers. IQ and intelligence have done this in the form of 'g' and, whether you agree or disagree with it, its ability to withstand the many attacks says much about its staying power. Ignoring it ignores scientific evidence and we do this for many cultural and social reasons, but it rarely leads to advances in our understanding.

Where to from here?

For more than a century scientists have had an enduring fascination with IQ and its correlates. Stating that there are differences between groups has proven a highly controversial topic. It is worth remembering that IQ, as envisaged by Binet and many since, was about individual differences and not group differences. This is where the research baton needs to be redirected. It is important to recognise and understand why such differences exist. Any psychological construct is only as important as its value, consequences and predictive powers. So how useful is intelligence?

3

Why do we care about intelligence?

Most of us had our first 'intelligence' test, of sorts, when we were born. Within minutes, midwives and doctors administer the Apgar test. This test, devised by Virginia Apgar in 1952, does not require pushing, prodding, needles or any kind of intrusive measures. It involves rating the baby's appearance (blue to pink), pulse or heart rate (<100 bpm to >100 bpm), grimace (no response to sneezing or coughing), activity (in arms and legs to all-over movement) and respiration (slow and irregular to good and crying). If the baby's Apgar score is less than 7 much more attention is given to the development and activities of the baby over the next hours and days. The claim is that the Apgar score predicts subsequent survival and development. In this sense, the Apgar score is valuable – it is not directly a measure of health, but a surrogate or approximation that is easier to obtain than plugging in heart monitors, using injections to draw blood and so on. The power of the Apgar score is that it unobtrusively measures and that it predicts. In the same way we need to ask in what ways a measure of intelligence (the IQ test) is valuable – what does it predict or explain? Is what it predicts useful? Do the positive consequences exceed the negative?

As we noted in Chapter 2, many psychologists and others began questioning the value of IQ tests in the 1960s and 1970s, particularly when differences in white and African–American students' IQ averages were used to justify race claims. Such disputes and discord led to a decreased use of IQ and intelligence tests, and alternative tests to identify differences in performance emerged. Many of these new tests were not successful, so the solution became obvious – devise a test that looks like an IQ test, smells like an IQ test and walks like an IQ test, and never mention the word IQ or intelligence. Examples include the Kaufman Assessment Battery for Children, and the latest revision of the Raven's Matrices – neither mentions IQ or uses the IQ scale. We continue to want to use notions of 'intelligence' but there seems to be a penchant to disguise this use.

It is certainly the case that in the United States, the country where outcry against the misuse of IQ tests was the greatest, there are a number of powerful tests being used to assess IQ but without a hint that it is IQ that they are measuring. For example, students who wish to enter a university in the United States must sit the Scholastic Achievement Test (SAT) or Graduate Records Examination (GRE) – both of which are standardised tests that measure, among other things, verbal and mathematical ability, the two abilities that are the major dimensions of many IQ tests. The use of intelligence tests makes much sense when it is noted that in the United States there is no common curricula across school districts or states. Any achievement tests used across state borders would then advantage one state over another (as must be related to one or the other achievement curricula), and thus is inherently unfair. Hence, more general reasoning, problem-solving and logic problems are included to neutralise the differences in what is taught in schools. It seems ironic that the country that most derided IQ tests, with many states banning their use, has one of the largest education systems built on the administration of IQ-based tests.

There are many claims for the explanatory and predictive validity of IQ tests. The value of intelligence is that it can be powerful in the understanding of real-life behaviour, and is among the most powerful predictors of many job-related performances. There are many other predictors of success, but few receive the same attention or have been as successful as IQ. A critical aspect to consider is that some dimensions of intelligence are more powerful in some situations, cultures, instances and on some occasions than others. Let us look at some of the ways intelligence and IQ tests can be valuable.

IQ predicts performance in jobs

The general argument often heard in workplaces is that different jobs require different skills and aptitudes and, therefore, that measures of specific job-related skills would be the best predictors of performance on the job. This is, however, not the case. As Frank Schmidt and John Hunter (2004) have repeatedly shown, this myth is not based on evidence but on wishful thinking. Rather, *general intelligence* is the best predictor of job performance, whereas tests specific to the aptitude required for the job appear to contribute little or nothing to prediction.

A great deal of intelligence can be invested in ignorance when the need for illusion is deep.
Saul Bellow

Having summarised the findings from more than 400 research studies, Schmidt and Hunter found that general ability was correlated highest for high complex jobs (17% of all jobs, r = .57) and medium complex jobs (63% of all jobs, r = .51), and not as high but still among the highest of all predictors for low complex jobs (about 20% of all jobs, r = .38). The best predictor of job performance is 'g', or whatever is measured by IQ tests. The more complex the job, the better IQ is as a predictor of that job! Schmidt and Hunter concluded that among the variables that can be used for hiring, none are close to general mental ability in validity (the next most valid predictor was conscientiousness).

IQ predicts performance in job training

Some have claimed that greater experience truly makes the difference to performance. Again, Schmidt and Hunter have shown that this claim is wrong. The relationship between experience and performance ratings is .49 for those who had been on the job for 0–3 years. This relationship drops rapidly to a low .15 for those who had been on the job 12 years and up, as Figure 3.1 shows.

There is a lot of evidence that a strong relationship between general intelligence and success at school exists. Brighter children learn faster, seek out more opportunities for learning and are quicker at choosing among a greater

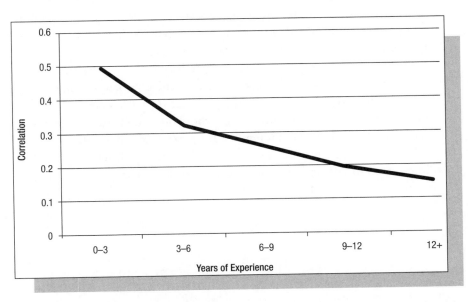

Figure 3.1 Relationship between years of job experience and performance ratings: IQ predicts and explains performance at tasks that require problem-solving

range of mental strategies to solve problems. Ignoring the substantial effect that general intelligence has on children's educational success can lead to major gaps in schooling. James Flynn (2008) has argued that the greatest shift in the past 100 years has been from schools teaching 'lots' of information (kings and queens, grammar, times tables) to problem-solving on the spot. Today's students need skills to think faster, think differently and think smarter, and such problem-solving needs to be applied more creatively to many new and often unstructured problems. These are the major dimensions as to what intelligence means today, and many schools are moving to developing these problem-solving abilities.

IQ can be used to diagnose problems

A common and valuable use of IQ scores is when a child is having problems with school work. Often these problems are manifested as the child being bored, acting out or not engaged. When such a child is referred to a counsellor, guidance expert or educational psychologist, one of the more valuable assessments to be used is a measure of the child's intelligence. A comparison between the child's actual achievement and progress when examined alongside his or her IQ can lead to specific treatments to correct the behavioural or academic problems. If, for example, the child is performing far below his or her level of intelligence, this could lead to a recommendation for more challenging and engaging work! If the opposite is the case, it may be that the work needs to be tailored to provide more appropriate challenges.

It is critical to note that it is rare for a psychologist to *only* use an IQ test – it is most often implemented as part of a battery of assessments. A study by one of the authors (Hattie, 1987), in the heyday of IQ tests, reviewed the files of more than 1,000 children from a large school district. There was not one case where an IQ test only was administered – it was always administered alongside other measures. Hence, the value of IQ tests is as much related to how it is interpreted in conjunction with other methods of assessment as it is to the score attained in the IQ test alone.

A great many people think that polysyllables are a sign of intelligence.

Barbara Walters

Intelligence is among the best predictors of earnings

It has long been noted that there is a relationship between IQ scores and later earnings. For example, Jencks (1972) found that men inducted into the Korean War who had high IQs (110+) had personal incomes 34 per cent above the national average after they returned to civilian life. In contrast, those whose IQ scores were below 90 had personal incomes about 34 per cent below the national average. However, it is not the case that IQ alone is the determinant of earnings, as commitment, motivation and opportunity are also involved. As we often note, when attending school reunions, it is often the students from the third- or fourth-stream classes who become millionaires and entrepreneurs, and those from the top two streamed classes who become the servants of these entrepreneurs (their lawyers, accountants and doctors). More than IQ is involved in earnings, although it is an important dimension.

IQ is related to the wealth of nations

In a fascinating book produced in 2002, Richard Lynn and Tatu Vanhanen outlined their theory that the intelligence of a country's population is a major factor responsible for national differences in economic growth and for the gap in per capita income between rich and poor nations. They used extensive data from various norming and IQ tests, as well as data from more recent international studies of educational achievement to estimate the mental abilities of 185 countries. Lynn and Vanhanen's work shows that differences in national intelligence have been an important factor contributing to differences in the wealth and poverty of nations from 1820 onwards. From their analysis, Lynn and Vanhanen concluded 'differences in national intelligence provide the most powerful and fundamental explanation for the gap between rich and poor countries' (p. 107). They then added two more variables into their equation, the extent of economic freedom and the extent of democratic systems, and these along with IQ served to explain 52 to 65 per cent of the relationship between IQ and wealth of nations – an almost unheard-of predictive explanation of the differential wealth of countries.

They provided two reasons for this high relationship between IQ and wealth. First, there is a positive relationship between IQ and earnings among individuals

A large section of the intelligentsia seems wholly devoid of intelligence.

G. K. Chesterton

within countries; second, there is a tendency for countries with a higher average IQ to have leaders (at least at certain times, such as Bill Clinton versus George W. Bush in the United States) who are also more intelligent than average; such leaders are more likely to provide an economic environment that is favorable for economic growth and avoid making mistakes in economic policy that retard economic development.

These results need to be treated with some caution because some of the data sources are questionable. To derive the IQ of a nation on, at times, very small sample sizes is suspect at best. For example, they used 80 students for Tonga and 80 for Western Samoa and both samples were children living in Auckland, New Zealand. It is also very difficult to believe a country's average IQ is 59, as was the case for Equatorial Guinea (with a sample size of 48 adolescents). This would mean that less than 5 per cent of the nation had an IQ above 100, and that if all the people of Equatorial Guinea were living in New Zealand they would all be in special classes. It is absurd to claim a country has an average IQ so low, based on so few, leading to such a ridiculous average. Something is wrong, for example, when it is noted that the overall average IQ score from the 81 countries listed is 88, well below the expected average of 100.

IQ and schooling

A long-standing debate has been whether schooling can enhance a student's IQ score. Many have claimed it is very difficult to make any changes, but others have disputed this. One claim is that schools can assist students to reach their potential (within the limits of their IQ) and others have claimed that there is no such notion as 'within the limits of their IQ'. Research by Cornell University developmental psychologist Stephen Ceci has exciting implications for schools. Ceci (1991) has demonstrated that schooling increases IQ scores. Teachers who 'believe' that achievement is more a function of effort and teaching rather than of intelligence are more likely to enhance their students' achievement (regardless of the correctness of this belief). However, it is likely that, while schooling may influence IQ, people with higher IQs may also seek more education and derive greater benefits from schooling. There is also a detrimental effect on IQ from dropping out of school early. Ceci (2003) described a study that showed

Advertising may be described as the science of arresting the human intelligence long enough to get money from it.

Stephen Leacock

a drop of 2 IQ points for each year of high school not completed beyond compulsory school age. Similarly, missing school (truancy, sickness) can lead to drops in IQ. This suggests that without the opportunity for mental activity provided by schools, intelligence can be significantly limited.

Concluding comments

While important, general intelligence (or 'g'), as measured by IQ tests, is only *one* of the attributes we value in our society. Arthur Jensen (1998: 356), for example, has underlined that the expression of intelligence in any person's life and in the character of a society depends on other factors, equally important, that are independent of 'g'. He goes on to say that it is the *interaction* between general intelligence and these other factors that accounts for much, probably most, of the enormous variance in the visible aspects of what most people regard as worldly success. Success in life is not at all related to a single factor; success has many dimensions and IQ plays an important part in only some of them. There are many other factors that can sit along with, and at times surpass, IQ and these certainly are valued just as much as IQ. These include conscientiousness, integrity, sustainability, effort, commitment and seeking to be self-learners, among other attributes.

Perhaps if we didn't use the terms IQ, 'g' or general intelligence we would be no worse off. Indeed, that is what psychology appears to have done since the radical days of discontentment about IQ in the 1960s and later. But this would be a false illusion, as we have reinvented IQ in so many new forms and words. Moreover, we still use tests (such as the Kaufman Assessment Battery for Children, the Weschler Adult Intelligence Scale and the Raven's Matrices) even though they have a reduced emphasis on the notion of IQ or do not used the term at all; we still assess children's generalised skills (under many names) before recommending various treatments and programmes; and we still find that general intelligence is the best predictor of job performance and success in many aspects of our society.

All men see the same objects, but do not equally understand them. Intelligence is the tongue that discerns and tastes them.

Thomas Traherne

4

The measurement of intelligence

We doubt that any expert in psychological measurement would state that the measures they develop or use capture every aspect of the psychological concepts they are investigating. Human behaviour is extremely complex to understand and to measure. One of the main problems that psychologists continually face is that the things they wish to understand are not always directly observable and therefore measuring them becomes problematic. This is in contrast to disciplines such as biology, where the biologist can name, measure and count different cells or organisms. Thus, the perennial problems of psychology can be stated as (a) defining unobservable concepts and (b) measuring unobservable concepts. Take, for example, the concept of jealousy. How would you define it? What is jealousy composed of, and how would you measure it? Sure, we all think we know what jealousy is, and perhaps have had a personal experience of it, but when it comes to defining what it is, then it becomes a much more difficult task. For the psychologist then, the problem is to ascertain a set of meanings as to what jealousy is, and to then devise ways of measuring these meanings. Again, this is no simple task. Straight away you can see that there are many things that the psychologist needs to consider before any measure can be built. As human behaviours, interactions and attitudes are complex things, any decisions as to how best to represent these are fraught with difficulty and controversy. Decisions as to what the set of meanings for intelligence will include need to be justified, tested and defended. This involves the processes of research.

Another issue to consider is that in choosing what to include in a measure other things need to be left out. From a technical viewpoint this relates to what is called *scientific parsimony* and it allows researchers to gain a basic understanding of the psychological concept being investigated. The issue here in relation to intelligence is that the set of understandings as to what intelligence refers to needs to cover the broader dimensions, which in turn capture as many of the smaller parts as possible. Thus, Goethe's claim about science leaving out important aspects of the phenomena when seeking to understand more about it has some legitimacy, especially in psychology, as we need to be as parsimonious as possible given the complexity of the subject.

In the early part of the twentieth century, the Harvard psychologist Edward Boring claimed that intelligence is what the intelligence test measures. In other words, intelligence tests only measure the skills required to correctly answer the questions on a particular test. It is not uncommon to find that IQ tests differ in terms of the types of questions they ask. It follows, then, that the types of questions asked are directly related to the test developer's definition of intelligence. Thus, a common critique of IQ tests is that they are too narrow in their focus and are therefore not a true reflection of a person's intelligence, but rather the test developer's view of what intelligence is. Boring's claim, then, is not without foundation as most, if not all, intelligence tests differ from one another in terms of the theoretical definitions and the questions they ask. So which of the many IQ tests available are the best? To answer that requires an understanding of the characteristics that a test needs in order for it to be 'the best'. It's time to introduce some technical terms to help you figure out what a 'good' intelligence test is.

What is psychometrics and why is it important?

There are two fundamental aspects to the measurement of any psychological concept: validity and reliability. Both validity and reliability are the *psychometric* terms that define the evidence required for a psychological test score to be of any use, from both a theoretical and a practical point of view. *Psycho = mind*, and *metric = measurement*, therefore *psychometrics* is simply *mind measurement*. Without the two essential building blocks of reliability and validity, a test and the scores it produces, regardless of its subject matter, can have no meaning or utility, because we would simply be guessing. If, on the other hand, a test has high validity and reliability then the scores obtained on it will have some meaning and can be used with confidence to make decisions about the test-taker. And

Many highly intelligent people are poor thinkers. Many people of average intelligence are skilled thinkers. The power of a car is separate from the way the car is driven.

Edward de Bono

let's be clear here, test scores are often used to make decisions about people, be they personnel recruitment, job reassignment and so on. Because they can and have been used to make very important decisions about people, the dependable use of test scores can have dramatic implications for individuals.

In many ways, establishing the psychometric qualities of an intelligence test, or any test for that matter, is like building a legal case in a court of law. One starts from the premise that the test is not guilty (has no validity or reliability) and then a case is built to show that it is 'guilty' of having these properties. Like any astute lawyer, a good psychometrician will painstakingly piece together a robust case to demonstrate that the test is worthy for its intended uses, and constantly be on the alert for competing claims that might undermine this case.

So, if a person gets a high score on an intelligence test, does this mean that he or she has high intelligence? It depends. The answer would be yes, *if* the test is valid and reliable, and *if* it has the support of good psychometric evidence. But many of the tests of intelligence in popular magazines, for example, have no evidence of reliability or validity, and therefore no weight should be placed on the interpretations from such tests. Such tests may look acceptable, but it would not be defensible to make any decisions based on tests such as these that lack evidence of validity and reliability.

Validity

In simple terms, validity asks the question, 'Can you provide evidence that the interpretation that you wish to make from a test is defensible?' A key source of evidence for claiming validity is that the total score from any test should relate to a single attribute. Consider that we have devised a test consisting of ten spelling and ten mathematics questions. If two people both get ten of these 20 questions correct, it is not clear what this score of ten represents. One person may have got the ten spelling questions correct and the other the ten mathematics questions correct. There is no way to compare the two scores as they derive from different attributes inherent in this test. So, an important consideration is that the questions in a test should all relate to the one single dimension. Psychologists call this *unidimensionality* (*uni* = *one*, *dimension* = *quantity*). So anyone writing questions to assess numerical word problems would want to make sure that numerical reasoning *is* the only ability being tested. A question worded 'Bob scored four tries and kicked four conversions; how many points did he score in the rugby game?' clearly has two dimensions: (a) numerical reasoning and (b) knowledge of the code of rugby and its scoring system. This particular question would, therefore, have a *bias* towards those who know how much a try and a conversion are worth. These people are using their additional knowledge of rugby to answer the question correctly. This sort of question is not fair and should never be allowed in a test because, as in this instance, not everyone is familiar with the scoring system in rugby. Therefore, one of the things a psychometrician does when developing tests is to check that each question assesses the construct (in our case, intelligence) of interest, and does not include questions that people answer correctly using skills other than intelligence (such as specialised knowledge). This is what we did in developing the IQ test for the television programme *Test the Nation: The New Zealand IQ Test* (which we discuss in Chapter 5).

Thus far we have claimed that a 'valid' test should be based on a clear set of understandings of what is being measured and that each question in the test should assess only one dimension – of course, we want this to be the dimension we are claiming to measure. Another essential component in the psychometric process is to provide some evidence that the test does measure what it says it measures. One way to provide evidence for this claim (and we used this method in *Test the Nation: The New Zealand IQ Test*) is to find an existing measure (gold standard) of intelligence and then correlate the scores from the new test with the scores on this gold standard. What you would hope to see is that people who score highly on the new test also score highly on the gold standard; similarly, those with a low score on one test also get a low score on the other. Any other permutation is not acceptable and would lead to evidence that does not support the validity of the test.

Reliability

Reliability, on the other hand, is about the consistency of getting the same score on the same test on different occasions. In other words, if someone were to take the test again would they get a similar score? The issue here is repeatability. For example, if you took the test the first day and scored 120, the next day and scored 85 and the third day and scored 105, the consistency of your scores is highly variable, and there would be obvious concern about which score, if any, to believe. In such a circumstance, we could say that the test scores lack reliability. The scores are so different

No one ever went broke underestimating the intelligence of the American people.

H. L. Mencken

it is difficult to capture your 'true' score. Which score would you think was your *true* score? Many of us would want to keep the test where you scored 120, of course! But, not so fast. We have to consider *why* the scores varied so much. After all, it is not expected that one's intelligence would change that dramatically over a three-day period, so what is leading to the scores being so variable? There can be many things that affect performance on a test; for example, you may be ill on one of the days, you may not have had your favourite breakfast cereal or you may have been nervous, and so on. The point is that scores on tests *can* change from one day to the next, and one of the key considerations in developing a test is to minimise these daily fluctuations – so regardless of where, when or how the questions are administered, the score that you receive from a test will be consistent, repeatable or similar over numerous administrations. Another way of saying this, but in language more often used by psychometricians, is that we want to reduce the unwanted sources of error. The aim is to minimise errors of measurement, or, in other words, maximise the reliability of the test.

IQ norms

Let us presume we have developed the test for *Test the Nation: The New Zealand IQ Test* and can provide evidence that the scores from this test can be interpreted reliably and validly. But we also need some further understanding of how we can compare our scores with other people's scores – how do the scores on our test compare with what would be 'normal' for the New Zealand population and how do we know what is 'normal'? This question refers to the notion of *norms*, which refers to the typical performance of a population of people. For our IQ test, we wanted to evaluate the typical scores (identify the norms) for blondes, left-handers and for all New Zealanders. There are some guidelines that can help us establish these norms.

One of these guidelines is that if we take a large enough sample of New Zealanders we can estimate the mean, and we can see how spread-out the scores are around this mean. We can also then estimate the average IQ for certain groups or categories; for example, by age, gender and occupation. One of the amazing features of most achievement attributes such as IQ is that if we obtained a large enough sample of people, then graphed the scores, we would find that there were as many people above the mean as below it, and that the shape of the distribution would be very symmetric. Please note that this normal distribution curve (as it is called) is *not* a stipulation of achievement or intelligence scores; it is a fundamental observation that psychometricians have found on numerous occasions. Let us look at this curve.

The normal distribution curve, or the bell curve as it is also known, does not *have* to occur, but with achievement scores it nearly always does. There will be a small percentage of people who score highly and a small percentage who have low scores, but the majority of people will be based around the average score. It has been traditional when developing IQ tests to arbitrarily set the mean for the population of interest (in this case, New Zealanders) at 100 and to create scores that then represent the various increments around this mean of 100. Similarly, we could arbitrarily decide on a scale for the IQ test (as was done when IQ tests were first developed in the 1910s). We could create scores along the IQ scale such that 50 per cent of the population is expected to score between 90 and 110; about 16 per cent would score above 115 and 16 per cent below 85; and about 2 to 3 per cent would score above 130 and 2 to 3 per cent would score below 70. Thus:

- An IQ of 80 would be higher than 10 per cent of all persons taking this test.
- An IQ of 90 would be higher than 25 per cent of all persons taking this test.
- An IQ of 100 would be higher than 50 per cent of all persons taking this test.
- An IQ of 110 would be higher than 75 per cent of all persons taking this test.
- An IQ of 120 would be higher than 90 per cent of all persons taking this test.
- An IQ of 130 would be higher than 98 per cent of all persons taking this test.

Figure 4.1 shows how this distribution works, based on a well-known adult measure – the Weschler Adult Intelligence Scale. It shows that about 2 per cent of any population would have an IQ between 55 and 77, 14 per cent between 70 and 85, 34 per cent between 85 and 100 and so on. There would be 68 per cent who would have an IQ between 85 and 115, and nearly all of us have an IQ score between 70 and 130. When we add the percentages from left to right, then 50 per cent have an IQ of 100 or lower, 84 per cent an IQ of 115 or lower and 98 per cent an IQ of 130 or lower.

Success in almost any field depends more on energy and drive than it does on intelligence. This explains why we have so many stupid leaders.

Sloan Wilson

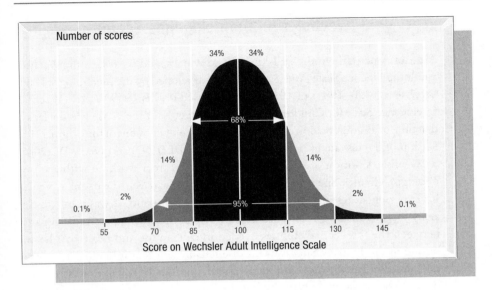

Figure 4.1 The normal distribution curve

As we found on the day after the *Test the Nation: The New Zealand IQ Test* went to air, many New Zealanders were surprised (indeed, shocked) that they had an 'average IQ'. Indeed, 50 per cent found they had average intelligence – which is exactly what was expected!

We have now discussed the main concepts that we would need not only to create the tests for the *Test the Nation: The New Zealand IQ Test* television programmes but also to evaluate the tests. Any scores from the New Zealand IQ tests would need to be reliable, valid, relate to one underlying dimension and have normative information in order for meaningful interpretations to be made.

Measures of adult intelligence

There are many current IQ tests for adults and for children, and it is impossible to provide the details of each, given the scope of this book. Any reader interested in locating a particular test should read the *Mental Measurements Yearbook* (http://www.unl.edu/buros), a compilation of reviews of all the published tests that are used throughout psychology, including many intelligence tests. What we will cover in the next section of this chapter are two tests that are often considered the gold standard for assessing adult intelligence – and which we subsequently used in developing the 72-question test for the second year of the *Test the Nation: The New Zealand IQ Test* television programme.

The WAIS (Wechsler Adult Intelligence Scale)

Arguably, one of the most well-known and widely used IQ tests is the Wechsler Adult Intelligence Scale (WAIS), which was developed by the psychologist David Wechsler (1896–1981) in 1955, and was based on his 1949 WISC (Wechsler Intelligence Scale for Children). Indeed, the impetus for the WAIS was the lack at that time of an adult version of an IQ test. Subsequent revisions of the original 1955 version of the test are to be found in the WAIS-III (1997) and WAIS-IV (2008).

Wechsler's notion of IQ stems from his early career working with the psychologist Charles Spearman and the mathematician Karl Pearson, as well as his experiences testing army recruits for job assignments. It was while testing army recruits that Wechsler became concerned with the apparent discrepancy between the intellectual abilities needed in civilian life and those that he was testing in the military. Such was his disenchantment that it led him to reassess his views on intelligence and its measurement. Wechsler believed that intelligence was not a single capacity but the sum of many different abilities. Thus, he set about developing a measure that provided some unique approaches to understanding and quantifying intelligence. Wechsler defined intelligence as the 'capacity of an individual to understand the world about him and his resourcefulness to cope with its challenges' (1975: 139). That is, intelligence is what we do in the real world and ways in which we adapt to meet the challenges of new situations. This approach was a radical departure from the staunch hereditarian views of intelligence as immutable, because it implied that intelligence was adaptive and could be changed.

In developing his scale, Wechsler provided not only a much more detailed and comprehensive measure of intelligence but also a more useful scoring system, as well as the notion of a performance scale. Unlike the other popular IQ test, the Stanford–Binet test (for children and adolescents), which required the test-taker to pass two out of three tasks in order to get credit for a particular test, the WAIS simply added up the number of correct responses to get an intelligence scale score and an overall IQ score. The advantage of this method is that groups of questions can be aggregated by content area, so that test-takers can gauge where their strengths and weaknesses are in the different subject areas (vocabulary, general knowledge and so on) as well as their overall IQ. Another advance of the WAIS was the use of a performance scale, which requires test-takers *to do* something other than simply respond to questions.

Talent wins games, but teamwork and intelligence win championships.

Michael Jordan

For example, they may be asked to point to a missing detail, or assemble a series of blocks. The rationale for the performance scale was that it overcame problems of test-taker disadvantage because of language, education and other barriers to performance.

Remember we said earlier that typically the psychologist will define a broader concept of what he or she is trying to measure and then find some smaller aspects to measure so as to provide evidence of it? This is exactly what Wechsler did. The WAIS is organised around four broader dimensions – verbal comprehension, working memory, perceptual organisation and processing speed – each of which has various smaller subtests, as explained below.

Verbal comprehension. The verbal comprehension dimension of the WAIS test has questions on vocabulary, on identifying similarities and asking for information. The vocabulary questions aim to test vocabulary level by asking the test-taker to define words. The similarities questions ask the test-taker to identify the relationship between pairs of words; for example, 'How are a shoe and a sock alike?' This section is aimed at measuring logical and abstract thinking. The information questions are typically general knowledge questions. The questions become progressively more difficult and are a measure of learning and memory. It is noted that such questions can be affected by cultural and educational experiences.

Working memory. The working memory dimension of the WAIS test includes tests on arithmetic, digit (or number) spans and putting numbers and letters into sequences. In the arithmetic subtest, all problems are worked out in the head and then verbally given. The arithmetic questions aim to measure knowledge of arithmetic procedures, concentration and short-term memory. In the digit span subtest, a series of numbers are verbally presented to the test-taker who is then asked to repeat the sequence either forwards or backwards. As the test progresses the sequences become longer. The aim of this section is to assess concentration and short-term auditory memory. For the letter–number sequencing subtest, both letters and numbers are randomly ordered and orally presented. The task is to repeat the numbers in ascending order and the letters in alphabetical order. Again, this section measures short-term memory and attention.

Perceptual organisation. The perceptual organisation dimension of the WAIS test includes subtests on picture completion, block design and matrix reasoning. In the picture completion subtest, a picture is shown to the test-taker, who in turn must identify what important detail is missing. This subtest measures perception, concentration, alertness and attention to detail. It is generally regarded as a good indicator of nonverbal intelligence. In the subtest on block design, the blocks are patterned in various designs using only two colours, and are placed before the examiner. A picture of a series of blocks in a certain pattern is shown to the test-taker who is then asked to reproduce the pattern. This subtest measures perceptual motor skill and psychomotor speed. It is also a very good measure of nonverbal concept formation. The subtest on matrix reasoning measures nonverbal analogy as well as reasoning and information processing. The task involves identifying patterns among a series of shapes. As the subtest progresses, it becomes more difficult to identify what the relationship is among the shapes.

Processing speed. The processing speed dimension of the WAIS includes subtests using symbols. In the subtest on digit symbol copy, the test-taker is shown a series of symbols that are associated with a number. The task is then to match as many symbols to the numbers as fast as possible under timed conditions. This subtest measures factors such as learning ability, visual motor dexterity, speed and persistence. In the subtest on symbol search, two geometric shapes are shown to the test-taker, who then has to find one of the two shapes in an adjacent search group of geometric shapes. This section is timed and is a measure of cognitive processing speed.

Scoring WAIS. A unique feature of the WAIS is the manner in which the test can be scored. Apart from a total IQ score, and the subtest scores (for verbal comprehension, working memory, perceptual organisation and processing speed), one can also compute a verbal score and a performance score. The verbal IQ score is computed using vocabulary, similarities, arithmetic, digit span, information and letter–number sequencing. The performance IQ score is computed using picture completion, block design, matrix reasoning, symbol search and digit symbol copy.

One of the reasons we chose the WAIS as a gold standard was that it has the most extensive psychometric evidence. The technical manual that accompanies the test is one of the most comprehensive that we have encountered over the years. Suffice to say, the psychometric qualities of the WAIS are well documented, suggesting that the test is valid and reliable and that the scores obtained from it are a strong indicator of the facets of IQ that it purports to measure.

To make a book is as much a trade as to make a clock; something more than intelligence is required to become an author.

Jean de La Bruyère

The Raven's Standard Progressive Matrices

The Raven's Standard Progressive Matrices (Raven's Matrices or Raven's test) were originally developed in England in 1936, by L. Penrose and J. C. Raven, as a measure of a person's ability to form perceptual relations and to reason by analogy. In other words, the Raven's test is independent of language and formal schooling and is a test of nonverbal IQ. It is based on Spearman's general intelligence, or 'g', and was used during the Second World War for military classification, proving to be most successful in predicting the performance of signalling and radar operators. Spearman's definition of 'g' was the process of extracting relationships among stimuli (question and answer). Thus, the fundamental aim of the Raven's Matrices is to assess test-takers' abilities to work out patterns, similarities or relationships.

The Raven's Matrices consists of 60 questions arranged in five sets of 12 questions each. Each question contains a figure of five to seven patterns with a missing piece. Each set involves a different principle or theme for obtaining the missing piece, and within a set the questions are arranged in

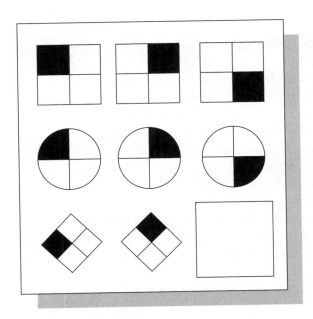

Figure 4.2 An example of a Raven-type item

You can't legislate intelligence and common sense into people.

Will Rogers

increasing order of difficulty, hence the notion of 'progressive'. The manual provides conversion from the raw scales to IQ percentiles, which can then be converted to IQ scores. (A percentile is the value of a variable below which a certain percentage of observations fall. So the twentieth percentile is the value (or score) below which 20 per cent of the observations may be found.) The norms are available for more than 15 countries but there are none for New Zealand adults. We used the US, UK and Australian norms and noted that there were only trivial differences between the IQ conversions from each.

Consider this example item (from http://wapedia.mobi/en/Raven%27s_Progressive_Matrices). You are asked to decide on the pattern to go into the lower-right-hand box. Typically four options are provided to choose from, but it is worth trying this version – note how you go about thinking of the right answer, how you have to see relations, consider options and invest some effort into these thinking processes.

Like the WAIS, the Raven's Standard Progressive Matrices have been thoroughly researched and have an abundance of psychometric data to support both their validity and reliability. Thus, it was a natural choice for us to use them in the validation of the tests for *Test the Nation: The New Zealand IQ Test*.

Concluding comments

To be able to claim a test has validity and reliability requires detailed evidence to suggest that the interpretations that we wish to make from the test has defensible evidence to support it, and that the results from the test can be reproduced on different occasions. If these things can be demonstrated through detailed analysis then test administrators and those being tested can have confidence in the results obtained and any subsequent decisions that are made.

With regard to developing the *Test the Nation: The New Zealand IQ Test* not only did we rigorously search for the best tests with which to correlate our test but also we employed some of the most sophisticated data analysis methods available to ensure that the test met the high standards required for validity and reliability. A detailed description of how we developed the test is given in Chapter 5.

I wish there was a knob on the TV to turn up the intelligence. There's a knob called brightness, but it doesn't seem to work.

Will Gallagher

5

The development of an IQ test

Both of us are busy teachers and researchers with lots of students, many research projects and a mutual passion for promoting our discipline of psychology and psychometrics. So when, in 2003, Television New Zealand called and asked us to meet to discuss the development of a New Zealand IQ test for a New Zealand version of the *Test the Nation* programme,* we were naturally curious and excited. The concept also involved having a studio audience made up of various groups who would compete in a live programme on a series of questions leading to an IQ score. At the same time, viewers could complete the test at home using pen and paper and an answer sheet available from various magazines, by answering on the web or by texting their answers in, and they could compare their scores with the average scores of the various studio groups. We worked on two programmes with Television New Zealand, the first in 2003 and the second in 2004. The programme is termed 'credible entertainment' or 'edutainment' and we were employed to be part of the 'credible' or 'edu' part!

The pressure on us was live television, 72 perfect questions, no New Zealand standardised adult IQ to relate to, no notion of the sample on the night and the average had to be a perfect 100 (which is the average IQ score)! The excitement was this challenge (and the opportunity to obtain and analyse the data).

---

* The *Test the Nation* concept is owned by Netherlands-based Eyeworks Holding and is licensed for distribution to many other countries, including the United Kingdom, Australia, Germany, Belgium, Canada, the United States, Indonesia, Denmark, Japan, Ireland and the Middle East.

The model for the New Zealand *Test the Nation* IQ Test

The format for the first year was based on testing six major abilities: language, number, knowledge, spatial awareness, reasoning and memory. Each of these components consisted of two subcomponents, giving 12 subtests (see Table 5.1).

The first dimension, language, was included because it is an important (although not the only) part of reasoning, solving problems and adapting to our current environment.

Arithmetic relates to how we handle concepts of quantity and numbers. Being able to add, subtract, multiply and divide numbers, as well as solve numerical word problems, are useful skills for everyday situations. For example, giving and receiving the correct change to/from the bus driver and being able to work out the time the journey takes is an important life skill.

Knowledge relates to the knowledge we need of how our world works, and includes both general knowledge and social knowledge (or social intelligence, as it is also known). Social knowledge (intelligence) can include the ability to understand people's thoughts, feelings and intentions; the ability to interpret meaningful connections among various acts of oneself and others; an ability to deal with people, to interpret sequences of social behaviour, to interpret changes in social behaviour and to be good at taking the perspectives of other people; and an ability to adapt well in social situations and to understand the common socially acceptable norms and rules in human relations in one's own society or culture (even if one does not follow these). Although social knowledge is one

Table 5.1 IQ test format, 2003

Dimensions	Subtest dimensions	
	Subtest 1	Subtest 2
Language	Vocabulary	Meanings
Number	Number problems	Word problems
Knowledge	General knowledge	Social knowledge
Spatial awareness	Spatial reasoning and object awareness	Mental rotation
Reasoning	Number series	Series completion
Memory	Word memory	Picture memory

I'm not offended by all the dumb blonde jokes because I know I'm not dumb . . . and I also know that I'm not blonde.

Dolly Parton

of the oldest notions in the history of intelligence (it was first well developed by Hunt in 1928 in the George Washington Social Intelligence Test, and was a key part of Joy Guilford's 1967 search for the 120-plus separate intellectual abilities), it is not usually included in the assessment of intelligence. The social knowledge questions in our test assessed knowledge of social norms in New Zealand society by asking, 'What is considered socially appropriate?' in various circumstances.

Spatial awareness relates to the proficiency to think in abstract ways. It often involves us reasoning in our minds about complex problems. Sometimes words help, sometimes they do not; spatial awareness is more related to solving problems while considering many parts of the problem at the same time. For example, furniture removal people often are faced with the problem of having to move awkward-shaped objects into confined spaces and, therefore, require spatial reasoning proficiency in order to meet the demands of such a task.

Reasoning relates to our understanding relationships and making connections that are not immediately obvious. The ability to reason through problems is particularly important when facing problems we have not seen before. The ways we think of possible answers, consider various options and reach reasonable conclusions are all part of what we call reasoning.

For our IQ testing, we divided memory into memory for words and memory for pictures. Memory is an important aspect for living and operating in our world. For this aspect of IQ we were more interested in the short-term memory. For example, it is very useful to remember where the car keys were last seen, or where children are to be picked up from, as there are important implications for not remembering such day-to-day things.

The questions

In the first year of the New Zealand television programme (2003), Professor Con Stough and his team of test developers (Karen Hansen, Gilles Gignac and Jenny Lloyd) at Swinburne University of Technology in Australia developed an initial 150 questions across six dimensions. Our role was to choose the final 72 questions, making sure they had psychometric credibility (high reliability), that there were high correlations between the questions and there was a standard IQ distribution of scores (validity), that collectively they cohered into a single total IQ score (unidimensionality) and that no question or answer would be challenged (credibility). We reviewed each question, modified many in detail, added some more New Zealand–based questions to the 'knowledge' dimension and pretested the questions. We then performed an extensive psychometric analysis of the questions to choose six questions for each of the 12 subtests within the six major dimensions of the IQ test format. In the second year (2004) we developed our own questions.

If you were to ask any test developer what the most difficult aspect of putting a psychological test together is, then more often than not it would be writing the questions. The difficulty is not only to write good-quality questions but also to write good distracter answers. Consider that each question has a stem (the problem) and four response options (only one can be correct, with the others being not correct but plausibly correct to attract those who do not know the answer to be tempted to choose them). The main issue here is that if you have four response options then there is a 25 per cent chance of getting it correct. If the distracter options are not too convincing then this probability starts to increase, but if they are well written then the probability of 'guessing' the correct answer starts to decrease from 25 per cent. The long and the short of all this is that it is the writing of distracter response options that takes the time and the skill to write. The last thing we wanted was for people to be able to guess the answer, as this would then have led to IQ scores being overestimated and misleading. For the 2004 programme it took us three weeks to write over 100 questions from which the final selection was made.

Criteria for choosing the questions

We used four criteria for choosing the best questions to assess intelligence in New Zealand: 1) item difficulty, 2) item discrimination, 3) item and test information and 4) identification of a common factor across the six dimensions.

Difficulty

We aimed to select questions across the *difficulty* range – we wanted some easy, some mid-range and some hard questions. But what does 'easy' and 'hard' mean? We know from the use of IQ tests over the past 100 years that, if they are administered to large enough samples, the distribution of intelligence looks very similar every time. Most people score near the middle, and of the rest,

We should take care not to make the intellect our god; it has, of course, powerful muscles, but no personality.

Albert Einstein

about the same number score at the top as score at the bottom. There is a sense of wonder every time a test of intelligence is administered – if the sample is large enough you get a normal bell-shaped distribution (known as the normal distribution curve) (see Figure 4.1).

Therefore, we knew we needed some questions that were of a difficulty level that best assessed people with an IQ of 85; more questions in the middle, to assess people with an IQ between 90 and 110; and some questions at the high end, to assess those with an IQ above 125. That is, we needed questions that about half of those scoring about 85 would answer correctly, so as to discriminate between those above and below 85; questions that about half of those scoring around 90 would get correct; and so on for every part of the IQ scale (from 85 to 130). You do not need too many questions at each IQ point (this would lead to redundant information), as the aim is to cover as many points as possible, and a long test may lead to fatigue during completion.

But this was a television programme, and one aim was to hold the viewers' attention to the end of the programme; therefore, we decided to have more easy than hard questions, while still ensuring that the final scores could be defensible when converted to the correct IQ scale (more on this later). So we aimed for questions such that the average score on the 72 questions was about 50. This meant that there would be fewer questions aiming at discriminating at the higher end of the IQ distribution, and thus we had to choose superb questions to discriminate those in this top half of the IQ distribution (>125 IQ).

Discrimination

The questions also had to differentiate between people with either a high or a low overall IQ – this is what is meant by *discrimination*. Difficulty relates to how easy or difficult the question is, and discrimination refers to whether a question can get maximum discrimination between high and low performers overall on the total set of questions – the greater the discrimination, the more power the question has to provide information about intelligence.

Information

The best way to choose questions is to consider the *information* (see Glossary for item information) from each question. The more information that can be gained the better the question will be able to provide details about its difficulty and discrimination. Another way of saying this is that the aim is to choose a set of questions that gives us the least amount of error in estimating a person's score (from easy to hard questions, from lower to higher intelligence). High information means low error, and low error means a large amount of information.

A common factor ('g') across dimensions

Across the various questions, and particularly across the six major dimensions of the IQ test, it is expected that there would be evidence of a 'factor' (derived from factor analysis; see Glossary) which explains peoples' performances on all the questions (whether they get questions correct or not). This is because we are saying that the 12 subtests are not independent measures of problem-solving intelligence but different measures of problem-solving intelligence and that together, each contribute to measuring what we are calling intelligence: the ability to problem-solve using language, numbers, knowledge, spatial awareness, reasoning and memory.

Choosing the final set of questions

Finally, there needed to be six questions measuring each subtest attribute. In some ways this should have been the easiest criteria to meet, but in reality it was not easy. We were essentially trying to do many things at once: choose questions for difficulty and discrimination along the curve that related to the overall score and that covered different components and contexts. We used a mathematic modelling process called linear programming to choose the questions to ensure that we met these conditions.

Collecting data for the New Zealand *Test the Nation* IQ Test

As noted above, we began the process of collecting data for the IQ test by reviewing the questions for appropriateness, accuracy and completeness. As a consequence, we made a number of changes to the questions. We then advertised on television and made contact with various factories, worksites and offices for volunteers – the aim was to get a group of people with a range of ages, occupations and abilities. The trial took place on a Sunday. The participants were administered the 150 questions, the Raven's Standard

The fool doth think himself wise, but the wise man knows himself to be a fool.

William Shakespeare

Progressive Matrices, and four subtests from the Weschler Adult Intelligence Scale (WAIS).

It was a fun day. Between subtests, the groups were informed about the purpose of each section, there were prize draws, a nice lunch and a gift bag at the end. It was fascinating for us to have a group of people so interested in the notion of IQ, and they certainly expressed disappointment when the day finished! The atmosphere during the actual testing was subdued and quiet, reflecting the attention being paid to the problem-solving, but the many breaks helped to reduce fatigue.

Altogether 274 people attended the Sunday trial of the questions. There was a greater percentage of females (62%) than in the population, but a good spread of ages (28% between ages 18 and 25, 38% between ages 26 and 40, 26% between ages 41 and 59, and 7% older than 60). The participants were asked to write down their ethnicity: 5 per cent were Asian, 7 per cent Māori, 3 per cent Pacific Islanders, 58 per cent Pākehā (New Zealand European) and 27 per cent categorised themselves as New Zealanders. It is thus difficult to compare with ethnicity from the census figures (because New Zealander is not an official census category).

Occupations were spread over a wide range. The most common were student (33), manager (18), retired (16), sales (14), mother/caregiver (14), accountancy/finance (10), information technology business (9), teacher (8), medical (8), unemployed (6), consultant (5), storeperson (4), receptionist (4), engineer (4), retail (3), restaurant (3) and legal/law (3). Other occupations included artist, volunteer, table game dealer, solicitor, seamstress, psychic, proofreader, plasterer, naval rating, meteorologist, ice cream truck driver, footwear buyer, dog groomer, celebrant, beneficiary and auctioneer.

We compared this spread of occupations with the New Zealand census figures. The sample included more service and sales, technicians and associate professionals than in the New Zealand population. There were fewer plant and machine operators as well as agriculture and fishery workers in the sample than in the New Zealand population. Table 5.2 gives an indication of how the New Zealand census divides up our workforce, and also a comparison with the Sunday trial audience.

Occupations were converted to a 10-point (low) or 90-point (high) scale to measure the 'status' of each occupation. Status is defined in terms of 'buying power' and is also known as socio-economic status. There were fewer higher (12% vs. 28%) and more middle (67% vs. 43%) socio-economic respondents, but similar percentages of lower socio-economic respondents (22% vs. 28%).

Table 5.2 Population distribution in the trials

Occupation group	Sunday sample	New Zealand population	Sunday sample (%)	New Zealand population (%)
Armed forces	2	5,892	.72%	.57%
Elementary occupations	7	61,926	2.52%	5.97%
Service and sales workers	55	90,729	19.78%	8.75%
Agriculture and fishery workers	0	104,061	.00%	10.03%
Plant and machine operators and assemblers	13	110,598	4.68%	10.66%
Trades workers	20	123,690	7.19%	11.92%
Technicians and associate professionals	66	123,885	23.74%	11.94%
Clerks	23	130,167	8.27%	12.55%
Professionals	42	137,517	15.11%	13.26%
Legislators, administrators and managers	47	148,989	16.91%	14.36%

The properties of the questions

We looked first at the attributes of an excellent question using graphical methods. What these graphs present is the relationship between a persons' ability and their probability of getting the item correct. Thus, people with more ability have a higher probability of getting the item right compared with those with lower ability. The graph of the performance of question 29 (from the original 150 questions) is presented to the left in Figure 5.1. It indicates that there is much discrimination between 85 and 115 IQ (−1 to +1 sd) (sd ≠ standard deviation; see Glossary for explanation), and the difficulty of the question is such that answering it correctly would indicate an IQ score of about 105. The steeper the line of the curve the more successful the question is at discriminating at the

Intellectual growth should commence at birth and cease only at death.

Albert Einstein

item difficulty (see Glossary) of the question. Contrast this with question 16 (to the right in Figure 5.1) where there is less discrimination (the curve is flatter) although the difficulty is about the same. Question 29 provides more information about IQ than question 16. It is optimal to choose a series of questions with steeper discrimination curves across the range of difficulty desired (80 to 125), and this is primarily how we chose the final set.

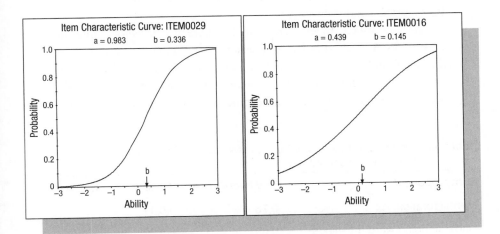

Figure 5.1 Item characteristic curves

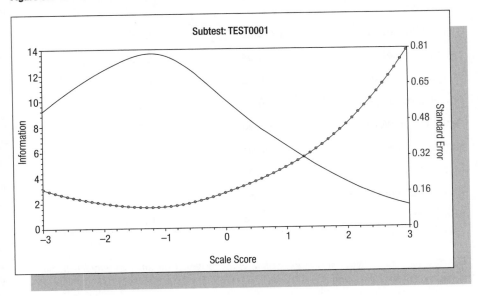

Figure 5.2 The test information function for the total IQ score (⎯⎯ = information, ⎯•⎯ = the standard error)

Using the four criteria outlined above, we chose the final test consisting of 72 questions. Figure 5.2 presents the *test information function* (our third criterion: see Glossary) for the total score (this is the accumulation of the information curves across all 72 questions). The least amount of error (i.e. the most information) can be found between 80 to 120 (this corresponds to −3 and −1 on the graph), and the least information above 120, although there is sufficient information to have confidence in the IQ scores across the range 85 to 135. The standard error increases for IQs above 125, hence there may be more variability in the IQ scores above this level.

We also wanted to evaluate whether there was a factor common to all 12 subtests. A method called *factor analysis* (see Glossary) allowed us to check this. We found that there is about 30 per cent in common variance across the 12 subtests. We found two clear factors (see Table 5.3) that were also very much related to each other. In keeping with the tradition of the history of

Table 5.3 Factors and their factor loadings for the *Test the Nation: The New Zealand IQ Test*

Subcomponent	Fluid intelligence	Crystallised intelligence
Mental rotation	0.78	−0.11
Understanding word meanings	0.69	0.03
Spatial reasoning and object awareness	0.50	0.01
Memory for words	0.38	0.20
Series completion	0.34	−0.02
Memory for pictures	0.22	0.20
Social knowledge	0.18	0.02
Arithmetic in words	−0.03	0.70
Number series	−0.07	0.68
Meaning for words	0.02	0.48
Arithmetic in numbers	0.33	0.42
Knowledge	0.26	0.41

The right half of the brain controls the left half of the body. This means that only left-handed people are in their right mind.

Anonymous

IQ, we called the first factor 'fluid intelligence' (mental and spatial rotation, memory) and the second, 'crystallised intelligence' (arithmetic, knowledge, vocabulary).

The notion of fluid and crystallised intelligence has been popular for many years (since Ray Cattell introduced the concept in his doctoral thesis in 1929, which was supervised by Charles Spearman, the originator of the notion of 'g'). Fluid intelligence (G_F) relates to the capacity to figure out novel problems, whereas crystallised intelligence (G_C) relates to knowledge that arises not only from better educational opportunities but also from a history of persistence and motivation in applying fluid intelligence to areas of learning. G_C therefore reflects more on scholastic and cultural knowledge acquisition. For example, it requires more G_F to answer the question:

Temperature is to cold as height is to

   (a) hot   (b) inches   (c) size   (d) tall   (e) weight

On the other hand, more G_C is required to answer the question:

Bizet is to Carmen as Verdi is to

   (a) Aida   (b) Elektra   (c) Lakme   (d) Manon   (e) Tosca

Persons with more G_F tend to acquire more G_C; that is, they reap greater returns on the initial investment of their fluid intelligence, and it is G_C that differs most across cultures.

The *Test the Nation: The New Zealand IQ Test* included both G_F and G_C. In Table 5.3, the numbers in each of the columns are what we call factor loadings and simply reflect the degree to which the subset of questions is related to the underlying factor: the higher the number the more the items in each factors are related to each other.

The tests with the greatest fluid intelligence loading included mental rotation, understanding word meanings, spatial and object awareness and series completion – all dimensions less likely to be affected by schooling or cultural influences (that is, whether the person is more collectivist or individualist). The tests with the greatest loading for crystallised intelligence included arithmetic, number series, vocabulary and general knowledge – all dimensions more likely to be affected by schooling.

Man has made use of his intelligence: he invented stupidity.

                                 Remy de Gourmont

Relating to the gold standard

Recall that a major aim of the Sunday trial was to relate our final 72-question test to the 'gold standard' tests: we needed to do this for validity reasons. The Raven's Standard Progressive Matrices was administered to all 274 participants in the trial. The average IQ was 95 (sd = 10.84), and the questions were very reliable (α = .89).

As the Raven's Matrices measure one aspect of IQ, we also administered some of the more verbal tests of the Weschler Adult Intelligence Scale (WAIS) – the four subtests of arithmetic, information, similarities and picture completion. In the *arithmetic* subtest the respondent must mentally solve a series of arithmetic problems. In the *information* subtest the respondent must respond to a series of questions that tap into one's knowledge about common events, objects, places and people. In the *similarities* subtest, the respondent is presented with pairs of words and asked to explain the similarity of the common objects or concepts they represent. For *picture completion*, the respondent must identify an important part that is missing from a set of pictures of common objects. We then scored these tests according to the strict guidelines in the manuals of each of the gold standard tests. All four subtests were very reliable (alpha >.73).

One way to tell whether the Raven's Matrices and the WAIS were measuring the same aspects of IQ or not was to correlate the scores. The correlation between them was high (.65), indicating that while the two tests share much in common, there is merit in combining the more nonverbal Raven's Matrices and the verbal WAIS to form an overall gold standard IQ score. Therefore, we combined the two IQ scores and the average IQ was 102 (sd = 18). This is very close to perfect – the aim was to have an average of 100 and a spread of 15.

We then equated the mean of the final 72 *Test the Nation: The New Zealand IQ Test* questions to this combined gold standard IQ. The average for the *Test the Nation: The New Zealand IQ Test* was 98 (sd = 12). The correlation of the final 72 questions with the Raven's Matrices was .67, with the WAIS was .69, and with the full gold standard IQ was .75. This score provides much confidence in any equating of the 72 questions with the gold standard IQ score. Scores were then transformed into IQ scores taking into account age.

We were now ready to proceed to the *Test the Nation: The New Zealand IQ Test* television programme.

It is the mark of an educated mind to be able to entertain a thought without accepting it.

Aristotle

6

Test the Nation: The New Zealand IQ Test television programme

The questions for *Test the Nation: The New Zealand IQ Test* had been tested and finalised – it was now 'show time'.

There were two days of rehearsals, with a group of Wellington drama students and their friends as stand-ins for the studio audience. There were many changes to the script, the autocue was constantly in a state of updating and there was lots of laughter as we worked our way through the programme format, inventing on the way, agreeing as to the comments and all the time trying *not* to use memory to rehearse lines as the aim of the game was spontaneity and credibility in our interactions with each other.

A major part of the entertainment was for viewers to see how the seven groups, somewhat stereotyped, would perform during the evening. In the first year the groups were: builders, teachers, students, twins, sports stars, blondes and celebrities; in the second year they were: models, real estate agents, taxi drivers, cricket supporters, Tolkein fans, 60+ and celebrities.

On the night the various groups were introduced to the format, and to the keypad boxes with A, B, C and D for entering their responses. The countdown began, and away we went – live to air.

As the test developers, we were anxious that the questions in the test would not be too easy – after seeing the questions on so many occasions over the past month, they seemed so simple! The first subtest was introduced (language) and then the first question – and there was relief when we saw that the percentage of the studio audience passing was very close to that of the Sunday trial group.

From then on, we were confident that the overall mean would be close to 100. Our concern instead turned to hoping that the studio audience did not detect any errors. If they did, it would be a sign that the folks at home would take umbrage at the questions and they could use any error to explain why their score was not an accurate reflection of their IQ.

As expected, the members of the studio audience felt very happy with their level of performance during the section administering the questions. This is not surprising, as when most of us choose an answer from four options we often think we have chosen correctly – there is no evidence to believe otherwise. So the mood was high.

Then came the answers. The mood changed; rather than the excitement and confidence that was evident when the studio audience was doing the questions, the air now was more subdued. We got through the night with no errors in the questions or answers, but there was some angst in the studio about a couple of questions. Many groups, except the teachers, forgot the basics of arithmetic. When asked a question like: $9 + 3 \times 2$ many put 24 whereas the correct answer would be $9 \times 6 = 54$. It seemed that many of the audience members had forgotten the age-old BEDMAS rule (brackets, exponentials, divide, multiply, add and then subtract)!

We know that telling others one's IQ score is akin to telling one's age, income and sexual peccadilloes. There was not much sharing of the IQ scores. A major reason for this relates to the major misconceptions about IQ. Too many people think that one needs a high IQ to be successful in today's world and then become upset when their IQ is not 'high' – they forget that there are so many other attributes that can make a person successful (such as creativity, perseverance, humour, personality). There is also a general belief that one's own IQ is somewhat high – certainly above average. We know from research studies that about 80 per cent of people state their IQ is above average – which is just not possible given that the tests are created so that 50 per cent are above average and 50 per cent are below average! This means that, by design, 50 per cent of people will score between 90 and 110, which translates into 2 million of the 4 million people in New Zealand classified as 'average IQ'. One of the aims of the programme, therefore, was to educate people on how the IQ scale works, and hopefully bring some realism into the interpretation

Sometimes I think the surest sign that intelligent life exists elsewhere in the universe is that none of it has tried to contact us.

Calvin from *Calvin and Hobbes* (Bill Watterson)

of IQ, as well as appreciation that IQ is but a part of success in our lives and that most of us do not differ so much from the norm in intelligence.

The final section of the programme involved reporting back the results. While some results were hinted at during the programme, the high point for the studio was receiving their comparative results. And, boy, was there a roar of delight when each group was revealed!

Profile of the studio groups

The competition for best group was tight throughout the evening. Figure 6.1 presents the IQ score for the seven studio groups. The celebrities were the highest-scoring group, followed by the teachers, who delighted in having beaten the students. The next groups were the sports stars, twins, blondes and then the builders.

The studio groups were *not* selected to be representative of all their populations (particularly given there were only 30 in each group) so these differences should be seen for the fun of the chase in the studio. Across most of the dimensions there were few differences in the average percentage-correct scores

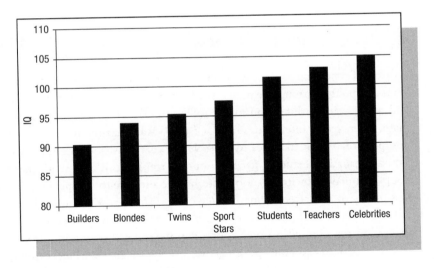

Figure 6.1 Studio group results, 2003

If anything, the essence of intelligence would seem to be in knowing when to think and act quickly, and knowing when to think and act slowly.

Robert J. Sternberg

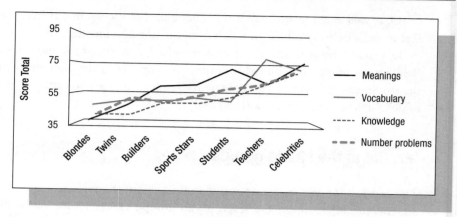

Figure 6.2 Groups' total scores on four dimensions where there are differences

for each subsection of the IQ test. There were only four dimensions where there was larger variability: The celebrities and teachers outperformed the blondes, twins and builders on vocabulary, meanings, number problems and knowledge – perhaps not too surprisingly, given that the former use these attributes often in their everyday vocations (see Figure 6.2).

Response to the programme

As part of reporting, the results from the first set of internet and text results from around the nation were presented. These preliminary results were engaging and created much discussion in the following days. The reaction was immediate, aplenty and interesting. Talkback radio was buzzing, mostly about the competition within families. When New Zealand is compared with many other international studies, it comes out on top in both competitiveness and cooperation. We may love to cooperate, but we also love to compete – and there was plenty of the latter during *Test the Nation: The New Zealand IQ Test!*

The reaction from colleagues was mixed. Many were pleased to see their profession represented on such a programme, some thought any promotion of the 'evil/outdated concept of IQ' was not appropriate and most thought it was fun. The hits on the Mensa website (http://www.mensa.org.nz) increased from ten a day to 9,611 the day after the programme, as did hits to a more

Some ideas are so stupid that only intellectuals could believe them.

Michael Levine

detailed paper on the development of the IQ test on the *Test the Nation: The New Zealand IQ Test* website. We have run special classes and adult education classes on our campuses detailing more about intelligence and IQ testing, and overall it has been a pleasant experience witnessing people's increased interest in measurement.

7

Profile of a nation

On the night, 180 participants responded in the studio, and 7,551 sent results in via the internet or by phone text. Each participant also completed a background survey, and this was used on the night of the programme to make contrasts and inform the audience about differences in intelligence.

As is the case with all statistical analyses, it is important to not treat any differences in the average of many subgroups as necessarily meaningful. An important consideration is how many points difference there should be before it is reasonable to conclude that the groups are meaningfully different. The answer in the current case, given the scale (80 to 135+ IQ), the sample size and the estimate of reliability, is that any mean difference of two or more points is worth considering further as evidence of difference (this is calculated using a statistical process called standard error). So, if the males differ from the females by 2 or more IQ points then we can be confident in concluding there is really a difference. Any difference of less than two is merely a function of chance factors (usually because of the vagaries of accurately measuring IQ). A further way to evaluate the magnitude of the difference is to calculate 'effect-sizes' – which is measure of the size of the difference – and in this book we consider any effect-size greater than .6 as substantial, between .2 and .6 is considered medium, less than .2 is small (see Cohen, 1969; Hattie, 2009). The 'why' of any difference is always the more fascinating consideration.

For each of the sections in this chapter there is a corresponding set of references for further information provided in the appendix.

The overall intelligence of New Zealanders

Figure 7.1 shows the distribution of IQ scores across all participants. It is clear that the IQ scores from this sample follow the typical normal distribution curve

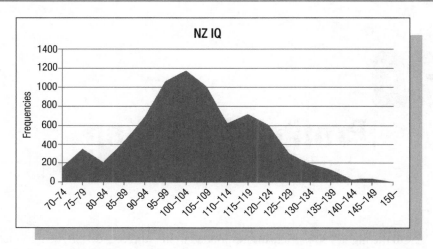

Figure 7.1 IQ distribution of New Zealanders

of the distribution of intelligence – that is, there are just as many participants above as there are below the average. The blip at the lower end is probably caused by a number of people who were under 18 years, for which the norms did not appropriately account (who probably called themselves '18 to 25-year-olds'), and because some viewers could have 'faded out' during the 2 hours of the test, and started to guess more towards the end – although this is somewhat ameliorated as they needed to finish the test before they could submit their answers (and the ratings showed no drop-off in viewers in the last hour of the testing).

Attributes of New Zealanders

Age

There is evidence that shows that as we get older (>40), there is a decline in intelligence, mainly due to a reduction in our processing speed and working memory capacity (Fletcher and Hattie, 2004). However, as we get older we can also become more successful in adapting our changing abilities to our

SCARECROW: *I haven't got a brain. Just straw.*
DOROTHY: *How can you talk if you haven't got a brain?*
SCARECROW: *I don't know. But some people without brains do an awful lot of talking,*
don't they?

The Wizard of Oz

environment, which takes some skill (a process often called selective optimisation: Ackerman, 1996; Baltes and Baltes, 1990). To allow for these age differences it is often recommended that the total score on the items is converted to IQ scores differently for the various age groups. There were differences in the total scores from the 72 questions by the four age groups. The mean for 18- to 25-year-olds was 52, for 26- to 40-year-olds it was 50, for 41- to 59-year-olds it was 48 and for those aged 60 and over it was 42.

Gender

There were differences between males (105.4) and females (103.8) – but, although males outscored females, the effect-size (es) was small (es = .11). This difference does not satisfy our guideline that there needs to be at least 2 IQ points' difference to begin to consider there is a difference worth interpreting. In the 2004 test, the difference was slightly greater (100.5 to 96.1). In both years, the subscales in which males outscored females the most were arithmetic and reasoning.

Height

There were differences relating to height, with taller New Zealanders the more intelligent.

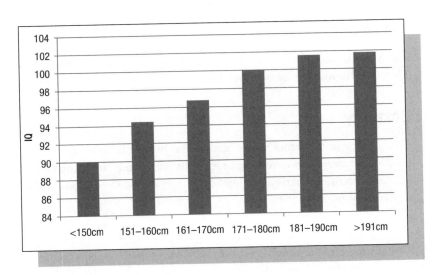

Figure 7.2 IQ score and male height

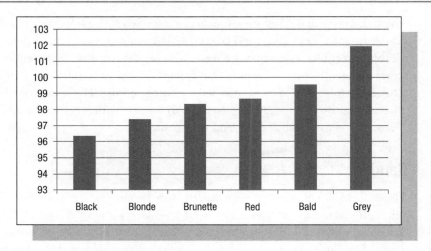

Figure 7.3 IQ score by hair colour

Hair colour

When participants and viewers were asked to *estimate* the intelligence of females with different hair colours, blondes were rated lowest, followed by redheads, with brunettes rated the highest. But when the IQ scores were investigated, there was no difference in these averages of IQ for hair colour; the pattern was similar across the two years of testing (see Figure 7.3). (This pattern was similar to that in the UK *Test the Nation* IQ results.)

Eye colour

This was the variable that was most systematic across the two years of the test. Those with grey eyes outscored all other eye colours (see Figure 7.4).

Dexterity

There were no differences in intelligence between right- and left-handed people, but those who were ambidextrous had significantly lower IQ scores (see also Corballis, Hattie and Fletcher, 2008) (see Figure 7.5). This pattern was observed in both 2003 and 2004.

Only in Britain could it be thought a defect to be 'too clever by half'. The probability is that too many people are too stupid by three-quarters.

John Major

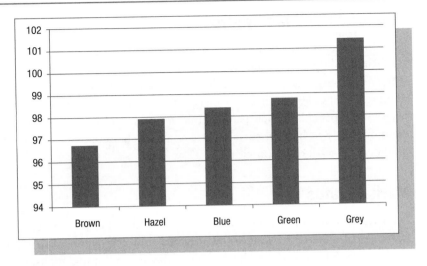

Figure 7.4 IQ score by eye colour

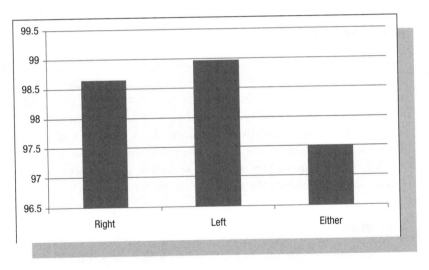

Figure 7.5 IQ score and dexterity

Glasses

Those with glasses had higher intelligence scores than those who did not wear glasses (99 to 96 in 2003 and 100 to 97 in 2004). The dimensions with the greatest differences were learning and language, with those who wore glasses outscoring those without glasses.

Birth order and family size

It has long been argued that being a firstborn and being part of a smaller family are related to higher IQ. The typical claims as to why there are differences is that (a) firstborns have more family resources available to them than other siblings, who by definition are in a larger family group, (b) firstborns experience longer periods of rich parent–child relations and (c) lower-IQ parents are more likely to have larger families. Despite such arguments, we found no difference in birth order (in either 2003 or 2004).

Marital status

Prior research has shown there is a marked similarity between husbands and wives in IQ scores – we tend to be attracted to others with similar levels of intelligence. Further, where there is more discussion among adults, there is higher intellectual performance (and vice versa). There were no differences in either year of the programmes for married, single or de facto relationships.

Books in the home

The *number* of books in the home (presumably being read and not just sitting on the shelf) has been shown to be a great predictor of intelligence – and such a question has often been used as a proxy to indicate intelligence when more formal IQ tests are not available. The highest relationships between the number of books in the home and the dimensions tested were with the dimensions of language, arithmetic and learning, and the lowest (close to zero) were with memory and reasoning. Figure 7.6 shows the relationship between IQ scores and numbers of books in the home.

Star signs

We know of no research showing there is a relationship between IQ and star signs. Further, we considered star signs over the two years of the programme, and the correlation between star sign and IQ was close to zero – again, showing that there is no useful information in knowing one's star sign and relating it to one's IQ. It is a non-informative comparison.

Intellectuals solve problems; geniuses prevent them.

Albert Einstein

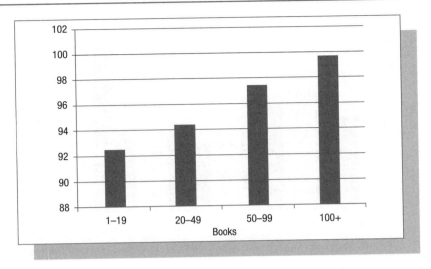

Figure 7.6 IQ score by number of books in the home

Owls and larks

It is popularly thought that people who prefer to work and think in the morning (termed the larks) will perform better at that time, while those who prefer to work and think in the afternoon and evening similarly do better work at those times (termed the owls). However, so far the research has shown that, despite their preferences, larks actually perform better in the afternoon and owls perform better in the morning. In terms of the results from both New Zealand *Test the Nation* programmes, there were no differences in IQ related to whether people called themselves larks or owls. There was, however, one major difference in larks and owls and it related to age. In both 2003 and 2004, younger people (18 to 25-year-olds) who considered themselves larks ('morning' people) had much lower IQs (92) compared with younger people who considered themselves owls (100).

Pet owners

The New Zealand *Test the Nation* data from both years indicate that those who had pets were no different in intelligence from those with no pets.

Food and alcohol

IQ scores were not affected by meat-eating or vegetarianism in either the 2003 or 2004 test results. But those who chewed gum had lower IQ (95) than those who did not chew gum (98).

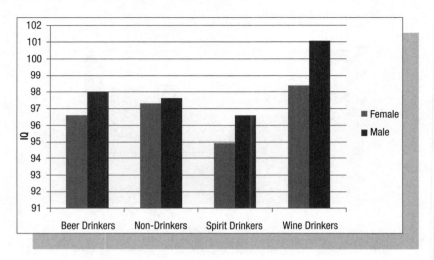

Figure 7.7 IQ score and alcohol

Those who drank wine (especially among males) had higher IQs, and those who preferred spirits had the lowest IQs. There were no differences between beer drinkers and non-drinkers (see Figure 7.7).

Those who drank spirits scored the lowest on the three dimensions that discriminated between drinking preferences. The wine drinkers were highest on learning and language, and beer drinkers highest on number.

Smoking

Those who did not smoke had higher IQs (100) than those who smoked (96). On every dimension of IQ, non-smokers outscored their puffing peers (see Figure 7.8). There also is much evidence that smoking in parents is associated with lower IQ in their children.

Sport

As Figure 7.9 shows, the most intelligent spectators were those who watched cricket and league, particularly when compared with those who watched motor sport and netball. There were some differences for males and females:

Intellectual brilliance is no guarantee against being dead wrong.

David Fasold

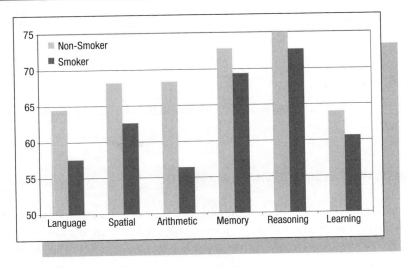

Figure 7.8 IQ score and dimensions of IQ by smoking

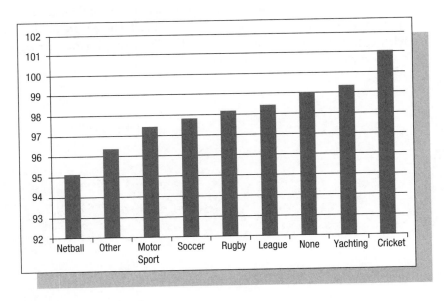

Figure 7.9 IQ score and sport

The difference between a smart man and a wise man is that a smart man knows what to say, a wise man knows whether or not to say it.

Frank M. Garafola

higher-IQ males tended to watch cricket, netball and soccer. This pattern was similar across the two years.

Exercise

There were no differences in IQ for those who did and did not exercise, across either year.

Summary: the state of the nation

As expected, the distribution of intelligence across New Zealand participants is normally distributed – there are just as many New Zealanders above as there are below the mean, and over half score between 90 and 110. The profile of the more-intelligent Kiwi was taller, grey-haired or grey-eyed, wears glasses, has more books in their home, drinks wine, doesn't smoke and follows the cricket and league. The profile of the less-intelligent Kiwi included being shorter, black- or blonde-haired, brown or hazel eyes, ambidextrous, drinks spirits, smokes and follows motor sport and netball. There were no differences relating to left or right-handedness, birth order, marital status, star signs, pet ownership or not, or whether you exercise or not.

The best intelligence test is what we do with our leisure.

Laurence J. Peter

8

The future of intelligence

Since our involvement with the *Test the Nation: The New Zealand IQ Test* television programmes in 2003 and 2004, we have had time to reflect on the programme's meaning and effect on the broader community. We started out wanting to be a part of a credible form of entertainment that was underpinned by top-flight psychometrics and, above all, remaining true to our academic traditions. We feel we achieved these goals and more, as the debate on intelligence IQ after both screenings of the programme was vigorous and challenging. We both feel that programmes such as *Test the Nation: The New Zealand IQ Test* are a valid vehicle for presenting contentious issues in a way that is both fun and educational. Further, from an academic perspective, the psychometric qualities of the two tests we worked on are as good as, if not better than, some commercially available tests. The tests we evaluated and made were created for the purpose of 'edutainment', and they have also provided us with a snapshot of IQ within the New Zealand context. The entertainment aspect is reflected in the bias towards easier questions based on the 72 questions, but still ending up with a test that had the expected normal distribution curve with a mean of 100 and standard deviation of 15.

The distribution of IQ was normal for the IQ tests that were administered in both years – this is not only desirable, but also a fascinating fact of nature and not an imposed statistical artifact. That cognitive (or 'thinking') dimensions are normally distributed is one of the most commonly found attributes of most human cognitive endeavours. There are just as many of us above as there are below the average in IQ when we consider achievement or cognitive attributes; just as many super bright as there are those at the other end of the normal distribution curve. Most important of all, the average IQ is 100, and most of us score between 90 and 110. It was amazing how many people taking part in the *Test the Nation: The New Zealand IQ Test* programmes thought that a score of 90–110 was somehow deficient – it is not: it is where most of us score on IQ, because this is how IQ tests are designed. It is as important to remember that there are so many other influences on our lives that are just as interesting, and that are predictive of behaviours and opportunities that we value (e.g. creativity, humility, openness).

Many of the attributes in Chapter 7 were chosen because of interest to a television audience and some could be considered of little scientific interest beyond a 'gee-whiz' reaction. Moreover, deeper analyses of reasons for differences on some of these variables would likely show that there are many interactions among variables that can affect the result (for example, interactions among variables may lead to different conclusions depending on age, sex, years of schooling and so on), or the variables may be correlates (for example, hair colour explained by age differences; grey-haired people are *more likely* to be older) that provide better explanations than if a variable (for example, hair colour) is considered by itself.

The variables that seemed to provide the most discrimination included age (younger participants had higher raw scores before conversion to take age into account) than older. There were also some social variables where there were differences in IQ scores, such as number of siblings, the number of books in the home and whether one was a smoker or non-smoker – such variables are often associated with more resources in the person's environment. There were no differences between males and females; no differences for birth order, marital status, star signs or pet-owning; and no differences between vegetarians and meat-eaters, or between those who exercised and those who did not.

There were two fascinating findings that were similar across the two years: those relating to 'larks' and 'owls' and those relating to handedness. For the first, younger participants who considered themselves evening people (owls) outperformed their peers who considered themselves morning people (larks). It does appear that our daily life is organised around three potentially different clocks: a solar clock, which provides light and temperature; a social clock, which relates to our preferences for work and play; and a biological clock, which we certainly know about when jet-lagged or have had too much exercise or partying. Generally these clocks are synchronised, but not for all of us. Adolescents and young adults seem to have the least-synchronised clocks and many make claims that they are better in the morning (larks) while other young people

Half of being smart is knowing what you are dumb about.

Solomon Short

claim they are better in the evening (owls). There were many more owls than larks in this age group, but our work and school life is not best tailored for owls. The greatest difference between these two groups is the extent of sleep each group gets – owls get far less sleep (especially during the week) than larks! Research has shown that this leads to decreased vigilance and attention (Goldstein *et al.*, 2007; Bonnet and Arand, 2001; Roenneberg, Wirz-Justice and Merrow, 2003). In the case of the *Test the Nation: The New Zealand IQ Test* programmes, the tests were administered in the evening (7.30–10.30 p.m.) and thus should have favoured owls, who believe they have higher arousal, vigilance and interest in the evening compared with larks. Indeed, this was the pattern shown by the results – younger people (those aged 18–25 years) who considered themselves owls had much higher IQs (100) compared with those in the same age group who considered themselves larks (92)!

The second fascinating difference was handedness. Michael Corballis has written many books explaining the genetics, differences and importance of handedness. We described to him the major differences we found in each year between right-handed and left-handed people compared with ambidextrous individuals. This led to a joint publication on this issue (Corballis, Hattie and Fletcher, 2008). There have been claims that various difficulties (reading, speech and so on) are more prevalent in ambidextrous people compared with those with stronger and consistent cerebral symmetry. The suggestion, attributable to Orton (1937), is that ambidexterity reflects a lack of cerebral dominance, which in turn leads to confusion over left and right. This can then be seen as a difficulty in reading scripts that demand consistent left–right directionality (Corballis and Beale, 1993). Orton also proposed that lack of consistent cerebral dominance could lead to conflict in the processing of language. Recent evidence confirms that atypical cerebral lateralisation can lead to such deficits as stuttering (e.g. Foundas *et al.*, 2004) as well as other language disorders (Lane, Foundas and Leonard, 2001). On a positive note, being ambidextrous may be related to creativity: Albert Einstein, for example, was an early slow learner who exhibited 'an unusual symmetry between the hemispheres' (Witelson, Kigar and Harvey, 1999: 2151), and Leonardo da Vinci habitually wrote left-handed in mirror writing, although he may not have been exclusively left-handed. Our data, however, supports the claim that there may be a dip in performance when people are ambidextrous.

Throughout this book we have referred to 'g' and to intelligence, and also introduced the Flynn effect, which shows that there have been major gains in IQ during the past century. It is worth examining the claims Flynn makes in his recent book *What is Intelligence?* (2008) to bring a lot of the research on intelligence into perspective. A major factor in the gains in IQ over the last century, claims Flynn, relates to the increase in solving problems 'on the spot'. Thus, the gains may be more related to *how* we know than to *what* we know; there has been little gain in school-related abilities (arithmetic, vocabulary, information): 'Today's youth are much better at on-the-spot problem solving without a previously learned method' (p. 22). Moreover, we have moved, says Flynn, from seeing through concrete pre-scientific spectacles to more abstract post-scientific thinking. It is not that our ancestors were stupid or that we now are geniuses, but that we have changed *how* we think: we have less difficulty now in freeing logic from concrete references, and are now more able to reason purely about hypothetical situations – and these kinds of questions are common in the IQ tests. Maybe we need to consider the various relations, abstractions and critical processes that are needed for surviving in today's world and using these as the criteria for building new forms of 'intelligence' tests. It is less 'what you know' or 'how you know' and more 'How well do you solve problems?', 'How sensitive are you to seeing patterns, abstractions and relationships?'

This suggests a future for intelligence and IQ tests – provided we are willing to acknowledge differences in what is being measured. We started the process of writing this book by suggesting that we wished to measure the cognitive and thinking methods that best allow us to cope with our environment. For many of the earlier decades of last century this could be measured by how much we knew – as this often reflected access to education and schooling, was valued in many professions (e.g. doctors, lawyers) and is what schools often valued (rehearsing and memorising information to pass end-of-year tests). I (John) recall, for example, my parents saying, 'Uncle Roy was brainy as he knew the Seven Wonders of the Ancient World'. I looked these up and memorised them in the belief that I too could become brainy! The message is not my naiveté but the notion that knowing lots was an index of intelligence. As technology allowed easier access to knowledge, its value (knowing lots) decreased, and we came more to esteem knowing what to do with this information. We moved to valuing problem-solving, reasoning and thinking about – built on top of knowing lots. As we increase the tools available to make connections, we may come to value more the evaluation and decision-making skills. Hence, measures of intelligence may need to move away from measuring our ability to know, to store much in working memory and to reason, and move towards

Man had always assumed that he was more intelligent than dolphins because he had achieved so much – the wheel, New York, wars, and so on, whilst all the dolphins had ever done was muck about in the water having a good time. But conversely, the dolphins believed themselves to be more intelligent than man for precisely the same reasons.

Douglas Adams

our proficiency to problem-solve, reason and, particularly, to do this quickly. In the near future, we may want to add measures of evaluative skill and optimal decision-making (often in the presence of many unknowns).

Indeed, this is how our measurement has changed. While there is still a case for using IQ tests of the past (WAIS, Stanford–Binet), there is a growing increase of new measures based on problem-solving and seeing patterns (and this latter is why the Raven's test has remained an evergreen measure in the history of IQ testing). The at times dirty history of IQ testing has brought many of the tests and their use into disfavour, but there are still many current tests that look like IQ tests, feel like IQ tests and are interpreted like IQ tests, but are just not called IQ tests. Instead we have 'assessment batteries', and the new Raven's is the same form of testing but now does not provide methods for calculating IQ scores. The claim of this book is that we need generalised measures of what we value in cognition and thinking. We need such measures that do not necessarily advantage those with lots of schooling or opportunity as there may be many without such schooling and opportunity who have the thinking skills but not the knowledge base. Why should only those who have been given resources and advantages in gaining knowledge be the ones to succeed (many of our current qualification and entry exams are still based on quantity of knowledge)? By using IQ or the more appropriately named problem-solving or optimal decision-making tests we can more readily identify those who could be taught to succeed.

Contrary to an often-cited and popular view, IQ is not immutable or 'fixed' by genetics. Again, James Flynn has noted:

> Huge g [general intelligence] gains from one generation to another show that IQ is highly sensitive to environmental factors, and some of these may be cultural factors such as learned strategies or problem-solving picked up at school, or at home or elsewhere.
>
> (1987: 33)

Similarly, Stephen Ceci (1991) has demonstrated that schooling increases IQ scores, although it is not easy to change them. Roberts *et al.* (2008) concluded that educational interventions can increase IQ by about 8 points – which could make a major difference in how we then apply these enhanced cognitive-thinking attributes to learning, to being selected into more elite

The essence of intelligence is skill in extracting meaning from everyday experience.
Ludwig Wittgenstein

programmes and to gaining the other wealth, health and happiness dividends that come from increased intelligence. But this also requires an investment of effort, and herein may be the true benefit. This should give hope to all that IQ can be enhanced in each and all of its dimensions. But note what it means to enhance intelligence. It means, for example, devising programmes of study and employing effective teachers who can enhance many dimensions of thinking. In James Flynn's terms, it means developing how we solve problems with cognitive content – that is, developing our mental acuity or the ability to provide on-the-spot solutions to problems we have never encountered before; developing our powers of reasoning to solve problems less in the concrete and more in the abstract; developing our attitudes to treat seriously the solving of problems, the acquisition of knowledge and information (the more you have, the more problems you can attack); enhancing our speed of information processing and developing our working memory. This can be accomplished but it should be clear that some content or context is needed to develop these thinking skills. These skills all assist in directing our investment of mental energy into solving cognitively demanding problems. The demands of 'intelligence' in today's society requires more than 'knowing much'; it involves having a sense of urgency in solving problems on the spot, and developing a persistence in seeking cognitive challenges.

What seems more important is to believe that we can make changes to intelligence, even when the research shows that this is not easy. Such confidence that we can change is the hallmark of many successful teachers. This is aligned with one of the major purposes of using intelligence testing; that is, to find people with high levels of skill in problem-solving who may not have been provided with the resources and opportunities to learn how to study or how to pass examinations, or who may not necessarily have been born into families who have provided the resources we need to develop our problem-solving skills.

Those who prefer alternatives to IQ and intelligence need to consider one of the major discoveries that begs for an explanation – that there seems to be some common elements underlying our skills in completing most cognitive tasks. Some may call this underlying skill 'g'; some, intelligence; some, working memory. However, denying it will not make this finding go away. There may, indeed, be multiple intelligences, but there are some well-established

The invention of IQ did a great disservice to creativity in education. Individuality, personality, originality, are too precious to be meddled with by amateur psychiatrists whose patterns for a 'wholesome personality' are inevitably their own.

Joel Hildebrand

commonalities across these many talents that beg for an answer – what is the nature of the core underlying skills that allow us to survive in our cognitive world? In this book, we are placing our bets on 'problem-solving', which can be taught, can be understood and is even more valuable when the problem-solving is in an area of worthwhile activity. Some would consider solving crosswords worthwhile; some, weaving; some, astrophysics and some, politics. We are not deciding on the activity but we are talking about the problem-solving skills. These problem-solving skills relate to the ability to reason, plan, solve problems, think abstractly, comprehend complex ideas, learn quickly and learn from experience. When these are mixed with personality dispositions such as openness to experiences and a tendency to engage in cognitively demanding endeavours there is a powerful mix of success factors in our society.

Intelligence is still one of the best predictors of much that we value in our society – doing well in school, doing well in jobs, health, wealth and happiness – but certainly we should not mistake one for these others, nor assume it is the only predictor. There are many other predictors of success, but few have received the same attention or have been as successful as measures of intelligence.

So where does the discussion on the development of the concept of IQ go from here? We would hazard a guess that the use of, and debate about, intelligence and IQ testing will continue in much the same vein as it has over the past century (although the terms may change). Debates will be hot about group differences, and these will be so strong that the power of IQ tests to account for individual differences will continue to be diminished, to the cost of many individuals who may be misplaced in remediation and inappropriate programmes of study. New jargon (e.g. processing power, critical thinking, evaluation proficiencies) will continue to replace older notions of intelligence, and new methods of assessing these attributes will continue to be developed (primarily because the cognitive attributes that lead to success in understanding our environment will remain of major concern in modern societies) and will remain important for a long time to come.

My view is that intelligence is the ability to use optimally limited resources – including time – to achieve goals. . . . The products of intelligence may be clever, ingenious, insightful, or elegant.
Ray Kurzweil, *The Age of Spiritual Machines*

Appendix

Some web pages

A great site by Jonathan Plucker and his associates is full of historical information and current hot topics, as well as resources for teachers. It can be found at: http://www.indiana.edu/%7Eintell/index.shtml

G. Scott Acton has a similar site that can be found at: http://www.personality research.org/intelligence.html

You can also test your IQ at various sites, but the quality of online tests are variable and should be treated with much caution:

http://www.2h.com/iq-tests.html

http://www.iqtest.com/

http://www.eskimo.com/~miyaguch/hoeflin.html

http://www.bricks-game.de/

http://unl.edu/buros

http://wapedia.mobi/en/Raven%27s_Progressive_Matrices

http://www.mensa.org.nz

Important books

Bock, G. R., Goode, J. A. and Webb, K. (eds.) (2000). *The Nature of Intelligence: Novartis Foundation Symposium 233* Chichester: Wiley. .

Ceci, S. J. (1996). *On Intelligence: A Bioecological Treatise on Intellectual Development.* Cambridge, MA: Harvard University Press.

Deary, I. J. (2000) *Looking Down on Human Intelligence: From Psychometrics to the Brain*. Oxford: Oxford University Press.

Gottfried, A. W., Eskeles Gottfried, A., Bathurst, K. and Wright Guerin, D. (1994). *Gifted IQ: Early Developmental Aspects – The Fullerton Longitudinal Study*. New York: Plenum.

Jensen, A. R. (1998). *The g Factor: The Science of Mental Ability*. Westport, CT: Praeger.

Khalfa, J. (ed.). (1994). *What is Intelligence?* Cambridge: Cambridge University Press.

Mackintosh, N. J. (1998). *IQ and Human Intelligence*. Oxford: Oxford University Press.

McArdle, J. J. and Woodcock, R. W. (eds) (1998). *Human Cognitive Abilities in Theory and Practice*. Mahwah, NJ: Lawrence Erlbaum Associates.

Neisser, U. (ed.) (1998). *The Rising Curve: Long-Term Gains in IQ and Related Measures*. Washington, DC: American Psychological Association.

Perkins, D. N. (1995). *Outsmarting IQ: The Emerging Science of Learnable Intelligence*. New York: Free Press.

Richardson, K. (2000). *The Making of Intelligence*. New York: Columbia University Press.

Sternberg, R. J. (1985). *Beyond IQ: A Triarchic Theory of Intelligence*. Cambridge: Cambridge University Press.

Sternberg, R. J. (ed.) (2000). *Handbook of Intelligence*. Cambridge: Cambridge University Press.

Sternberg, R. J. (ed.) (2002). *Why Smart People Can Be So Stupid*. New Haven: Yale University Press.

Sternberg, R. J. and Detterman, D. K. (eds) (1986). *What is Intelligence? Contemporary Viewpoints on its Nature and Definition*. Norwood, NJ: Ablex.

Sternberg, R. J. and Grigorenko, E. L. (2002). *The General Factor of Intelligence: How General is It?* Mahwah, NJ: Lawrence Erlbaum.

Sternberg, R. J. and Kaufman, J. C. (eds) (2001). *The Evolution of Intelligence*. Mahwah, NJ: Lawrence Erlbaum.

Valencia, R. R. and Suzuki, L. A. (2001). *Intelligence Testing and Minority Students: Foundations, Performance Factors, and Assessment Issues*. Thousand Oaks, CA: Sage.

IQ tests and their use

Jencks, C. (1972). *Inequality: A Reassessment of the Effect of Family and Schooling in America*. New York: Harper & Row.

Jensen, A. R. (1969). How much can we boost I.Q. and scholastic achievement? *Harvard Educational Review, 33*, 1–123.

Jensen, A. R. (1998). *The g Factor: The Science of Mental Ability*. Westport, CT: Praeger.

Kaufman, A. S. (1990) *Assessing Adolescent and Adult Intelligence*. Boston: Allyn and Bacon.

Kaufman, A. S. (1994) *Intelligent Testing with the WISC-III*. New York: John Wiley.

Linn, R. (ed.) (1989) *Intelligence: Measurement, Theory, and Public Policy. Proceedings of a Symposium in Honor of Lloyd G. Humphries*. Urbana: University of Illinois Press.

Love, H. D. (1990) *Assessment of Intelligence and Development of Infants and Young Children with Specialized Measures*. Springfield, IL: Charles C. Thomas.

Mensh, E. and Mensh, H. (1991) *The IQ Mythology: Class, Race, Gender, and Inequality*. Carbondale, IL: Southern Illinois University Press.

Sprandel, H. Z. (1995) *The Psychoeducational Use and Interpretation of the Wechsler Adult Intelligence Scale* (2nd edn). Springfield, IL: Charles C. Thomas.

Common beliefs about IQ

Derr, R. (1989). Insights on the nature of intelligence from ordinary discourse. *Intelligence, 13*, 113–18.

Gottfredson, L. S. (1997). Mainstream science on intelligence: An editorial with 52 signatories, history, and bibliography. *Intelligence, 24*, 13–23.

Sternberg, R. J., Conway, B. E., Ketron, J. L. and Bernstein, M. (1981). People's conceptions of intelligence. *Journal of Personality and Social Psychology, 41*, 370–85.

Relationships to intelligence

Heredity

Although the largest contributor to intelligence may be heredity, the effects of environment have been greatly underestimated – particularly how environment leads to opportunities, encouragement and basic living quality. It is, however, the interaction of the effects of genetics and environment that is most powerful. It is likely that there are as many people genetically well endowed with IQ who live in poverty, have little access to schooling and have been given few opportunities to learn as there are people genetically less endowed with IQ-ruling nations and living in excess.

Dickens, W. T. and Flynn, J. R. (2001). Heritability estimates versus large environmental effects: The IQ paradox resolved. *Psychological Review, 108*(2), 346–69.

Grigorenko, E. I. (2000). Heritability and intelligence. In R. Sternberg (ed.), *Handbook of Intelligence* (pp. 53–87). New York: Cambridge University Press.

Herrnstein, R. and Murray, C. (1994) *The Bell Curve: Intelligence and Class Structure in American Life*. New York: Free Press.

Studies of twins

Research on twins still dominates recent research on intelligence. There remains much controversy, but some findings seem well supported. Monozygotic twins (MZ twins from the same egg) reared together are much more similar in IQ (r = .86) than dizygotic twins (DZ twins from different eggs) reared together (.60). MZ twins reared apart (r =.75) are more similar in IQ than DZ twins reared together (r = .60). The relation between siblings is about .50. The IQ of adopted persons who have never known their biological parents is more highly related with the IQ of their biological parents than with the IQ of their adoptive parents. Unrelated persons reared together from infancy show a much lower IQ relationship with each other (r = .25 in childhood and r = −.01 in adulthood) than do biological siblings reared together (r = .49). So, IQs of twins are closer than between non-twins within a family – regardless of the family in which they are reared.

Detterman, D. K., Thompson, L. A. and Plomin, R. (1990). Genetics of specific cognitive abilities. *Annual Review of Genetics, 20*, 369–84.

Changing a person's IQ

Stephen Ceci (1991) has demonstrated that schooling increases IQ scores, although it is difficult to find many specific or short-term programmes that make a difference to IQ scores. Teachers who believe that achievement is more a function of effort and teaching than of intelligence are more likely to enhance their student's achievement (regardless of the correctness of this belief). It is likely that, while schooling may influence IQ, people with higher IQs may also seek more education and derive greater benefits from schooling.

There is a detrimental effect on IQ from dropping out of school early. Ceci (2003) described a study that showed a drop of 2 IQ points for each year of high school not completed beyond compulsory school age. Similarly, missing school (truancy, sickness) can lead to drops in IQ. This suggests that without the opportunity for mental activity provided by schools, intelligence can be significantly limited.

Ceci, S. (1991). How much does schooling influence general intelligence and its cognitive components? A reassessment of the evidence. *Developmental Psychology*, *37*, 703–22.

Dickens, W. T. and Flynn, J. R. (2001). Heritability estimates versus large environmental effects: The IQ paradox resolved. *Psychological Review, 108(2)*, 346–69.

Grotzer, T. and Perkins, D. N. (2000). Teaching intelligence. In R. Sternberg (ed.), *Handbook of Intelligence* (pp. 492–515). New York: Cambridge University Press.

Self-ratings of IQ scores

There is only a modest correlation between self-estimated IQ and actual IQ score. Nearly everyone estimates that their IQ is above 100 (the average IQ scores from reputable tests). Males give a higher mean self-estimate of IQs than do females (113 vs. 106), and male estimates are significantly higher than their actual IQ and female estimates are significantly lower than their actual IQ. Females attribute higher IQs to others than they claim for themselves, whereas males attribute lower IQs to others than for themselves. Females estimated higher IQs for their fathers than for their mothers (114 vs. 107).

Bennett, M. (1996). Men's and women's self-estimates of intelligence. *Journal of Social Psychology*, *136*, 411–12.

Furnham, A. and Rawles, R. (1999). Correlations between self-estimated and psychometrically measured IQ. *Journal of Social Psychology*, *39(4)*, 405–10.

Furnham, A., Clark, K. and Bailey, K. (1999). Sex differences in estimates of multiple intelligences. *European Journal of Personality*, *13*, 247–59.

Furnham, A., Dixon, D., Harrison, T., Rasmussen, S. and O'Connor, R. (2000.). Sex, social class, and estimating IQ: Middle-class male subjects rate themselves most intelligent. *Psychological Reports*, *87(3)*, 753–8.

Hogan, H. W. (1978). IQ self-estimates of males and females. *Journal of Social Psychology*, *106(1)*, 137–8.

Reilly, J. and Mulhern, G. (1993). Gender differences in self-estimated IQ: The need for care in interpreting group data. *Personality and Individual Differences*, *18(2)*, 189–92.

Changes over generations

Deary (2000) reported a study where 101 children who were tested for intelligence in 1932 at age 11 were retested in 1998 at age 77. The correlation between the two scores was a staggering .77 – that is, a person high in intelligence at age 11 is most likely to be high in intelligence at age 77, and similarly for those low in intelligence! James Flynn's demonstration that there is an average increase of over three IQ points per decade was found for virtually every type of intelligence test, delivered to nearly every type of group. For example, Flynn concluded that someone who scored among the strongest 10 per cent in the Raven's Matrices a hundred years ago would nowadays be categorised among the weakest 5 per cent. The Flynn effect can account for some of the reduction of IQ with age, as older people were raised in a period where the general level of intelligence was lower. Flynn argues that it is probably not intelligence itself that is increasing but some kind of abstract problem-solving ability. It may, however, be that because people are more exposed to testing, and in particular IQ type tests, IQ scores are changing. Perhaps IQ scores may increase as a function of watching and taking part in television programmes such as *Test the Nation: The New Zealand IQ Test*. Who knows?

Flynn, J. R. (1984). *The Mean IQ of Americans: Massive Gains.* New York: Harper & Row.

Flynn, J. R. (1987). Massive IQ gains in 14 nations: What IQ tests really measure. *Psychological Bulletin, 101*, 171–91.

Flynn, J. R. (2007). *What is Intelligence? Beyond the Flynn Effect.* Cambridge: Cambridge University Press.

Neisser, U. (1977). Rising scores on intelligence tests. *American Scientist* (September–October).

Context

Birth order and family size

Page, E. B. and Grandon, G. (1979). Family configuration and mental ability: Two theories contrasted with U.S. data. *American Educational Research Journal, 16*, 257–72.

Rodgers, J. L., Harrington, G. H., van den Gord, E. and Ross, D. C. (2000). Resolving the debate over birth order, family size, and intelligence. *American Psychology, 55(6)*, 599–612.

Zajonc, R. B. and Mullally, P. R. (1997). Birth order: Reconciling conflicting effects. *American Psychology, 52*, 683–99.

Married, de facto and single status

Dixon, R. A. and Gould, O. S. (1996). Adults telling and retelling stories collaboratively. In P. B. Baltes and U. M. Staudinger (eds), *Interactive Minds:*

Life-Span Perspective on the Social Foundation of Cognition (pp. 221–41). New York: Cambridge University Press.

Mascie-Taylor, C. G. N., Harrison, G. A., Hiorns, R. W. and Gibson, J. B. (1987). Husband–wife similarities in different components of the WAIS IQ test. *Journal of Biosocial Science, 19,* 149–55.

Life expectancy

Those with higher IQs at age 11 are more likely to live longer than those with lower IQs at age 11.

Whatley, L. and Deary, I. (2001). Longitudinal cohort study of childhood IQ and survival up to age 76. *British Medical Journal, 322(7290),* 819–911.

Occupation

Success in occupations depends on many cognitive and learned skills, which may be influenced by IQ among other attributes. IQ is related to occupation to the degree that the occupation requires abstract reasoning and problem-solving. Those occupations with lower mean IQ levels also have the largest variability. For example, farmers have an average IQ of 93 but the largest range of IQ (from < 50 up to 150).

Hunter, J. E. and Schmidt, F. L. (1996). Intelligence and job performance: Economic and social implications. *Psychology, Public Policy, and Law, 2,* 447–72.

Hunter, J. E., Schmidt, F. L. and Judiesch, M. K. (1990). Individual differences in output variability as a function of job complexity. *Journal of Applied Psychology, 75,* 28–42.

Schmidt, F. L. (1988). The problem of group differences in ability scores in employment selection. *Journal of Vocational Behavior, 33,* 272–92.

Schmidt, F. L., Ones, D. S. and Hunter, J. E. (1992). Personnel selection. *Annual Review of Psychology, 43,* 627–70.

Attributes of individuals

Age

Ackerman, P. L. (1996). A theory of adult intellectual development, process, personality, interests and knowledge. *Intelligence, 22,* 227–57.

Baltes, P. B. and Baltes, M. M. (1990). Psychological perspectives on successful aging: The model of selective optimisation with compensation. In P. B. Baltes and M. M. Baltes (eds), *Successful Aging: Perspectives from the Behavioural Science* (pp. 1–34). New York: Cambridge University Press.

Berg, C. A. (2000). Intellectual development in adulthood. In R. Sternberg (ed.), *Handbook of Intelligence* (pp. 117–37). New York: Cambridge University Press.

Bigler, E., Johnson, S., Jackson, C. and Blatter, D. (1995). Aging, brain size, and IQ. *Intelligence, 21,* 109–19.

Sex differences

Colom, R., Juan-Espinosa, M., Abad, F. and Garcia, L.F. (2000). Negligible sex differences in general intelligence. *Intelligence, 27,* 57–68

Lynn, R. (1994). Sex differences in intelligence and brain size: A paradox resolved. *Personality and Individual Differences, 17(2),* 257–71.

Mackintosh, N. J. (1997). Sex differences and IQ. *Journal of Biosocial Science, 28(4),* 559–71.

Nutrition (height and weight)

The best-established health correlates are stature (taller people are brighter), head size, brain size, frequency of brainwaves, speed of evoked brain potentials, rate of brain glucose metabolism and general health.

James, W. H. (1982). The IQ advantage of the heavier twin. *British Journal of Psychology, 73(4),* 513–17.

Lagerstroem, M., Bremme, K., Encroth, P. and Magnusson, D. (1991). School performance and IQ test scores at age 13 as related to birth weight and gestational age. *Scandinavian Journal of Psychology, 32(4),* 316–24.

Lynn, R. (1989). A nutrition theory of the secular increases in intelligence: Positive correlations between height, head size and IQ. *British Journal of Educational Psychology, 59(3),* 372–7.

Matte, T. D., Bresnahan, M., Begg, M. D. and Susser, E. (2001). Influence of variation in birth weight within normal range and within siblings on IQ at age 7 years: Cohort study. *British Medical Journal, 323(7308),* 310–14.

Segal, N. I. (1989). Origins and implications of handedness and relative birth weight for IQ in monozygotic twin pairs. *Neuropsychologia, 27(4),* 349–61.

Head size

There is a slight positive correlation (r = .20) between head size and IQ scores. Head size is a proxy for brain size, and the correlation with brain size is in the .30 to .40 range. Phillippe Rushton (1995) found that African-descended peoples average cranial size was 1267 cm^3, European-descended peoples was 1347 cm^3 and East Asian-descended peoples was 1364 cm^3. He hypothesised that these differences, containing millions of brain cells and hundreds of millions of synapses, underlie the race differences in IQ. This is a very contentious and much-argued claim.

Jensen, A. R. and Johnson, F. W. (1994). Race and sex differences in head size and IQ. *Intelligence, 18*, 309–33.

Lynn, R. (1989). A nutrition theory of the secular increases in intelligence: Positive correlations between height, head size and IQ. *British Journal of Educational Psychology, 59(3)*, 372–77.

Rushton, J. P. (1995). *Race, evolution and behavior: A life history perspective.* Port Huron, MI: Charles Darwin Research Institute.

Vernon, P. A., Wickett, J. C., Bazana, G. and Stelmack, R. M. (2000). The neuropsychology and psychophysiology of human intelligence. In R. Sternberg (ed.), *Handbook of Intelligence* (pp. 241–64). New York: Cambridge University Press.

Willerman, L., Schultz, R., Rutledge, H. N. and Bigler, E. (1991). *In vivo* brain size and intelligence. *Intelligence, 15*, 223–38.

Hair colour

Weir, W. and Pine-Davis, M. (1989). 'Dumb blondes' and 'temperamental redheads'. The effects of hair colour on some attributed personality characteristics of women. *Irish Journal of Psychology, 10(1)*, 11–19.

Alcohol

Oscar-Berman, M., Clancy, J. P. and Weber, D. A. (1993). Discrepancies between IQ and memory scores in alcoholism and ageing. *Clinical Neuropsychologist*, 7(3), 281–96.

Streissguth, A. P., Barr, H. M. and Sampson, P. D. (1990). Moderate prenatal alcohol exposure: Effects on child IQ and learning problems at age 712 years. *Alcoholism: Clinical and Experimental Research, 14(5)*, 662–9.

Larks or owls: preference for time of day for 'thinking'

Bonnet, M. H. and Arand, D. L. (2001). Impact of activity and arousal upon spectral EEG parameters. *Physiology & Behavior*, *74*, 291–8.

Goldstein, D., Hahn, C. S., Hasher, L., Wiprzycka, U. and Zelazo, P. D. (2007). Time of day, intellectual performance, and behavioral problems in morning versus evening type adolescents: Is there a synchrony effect? *Personality and Individual Differences*, *42(3)*, 431–40

Gupta, S. (1991). Effects of time of day and personality on intelligence test scores. *Personality and Individual Differences*, *12(11)*, 1227–31.

Leigh, C. and Reynolds, C. R. (1982). Morning versus afternoon testing and children's intelligence test performance. *Perceptual and Motor Skills*, *55(1)*, 93–4.

Roenneberg, T., Wirz-Justice, A. and Merrow, M. (2003). Life between the clocks: Daily temporal patterns of human chronotypes. *Journal of Biological Rhythms*, *18*, 80–90.

Song, J. and Stough, C. (2000). The relationship between morningness-eveningness, time-of-day, speed of information processing, and intelligence. *Personality and Individual Differences*, *29(6)*, 1179–90.

Handedness

Corballis, M. C. (1997). The genetics and evolution of handedness. *Psychological Review*, *104*, 714–27.

Corballis, M. C. and Beale, I. L. (1993). Orton revisited: Dyslexia, laterality, and left–right confusion. In D. M. Willows, R. S. Kruk and E. Corcos (eds), *Visual Processes in Reading and Reading Disabilities* (pp. 57–73). Hillsdale, NJ: Lawrence Erlbaum.

Corballis, M. C., Hattie, J. and Fletcher, R. (2008). Handedness and intellectual achievement: An even-handed look. *Neuropsychologia*, *46*, 374–8.

Foundas, A. L., Bollich, A. M., Feldman, J., Corey, D. M., Hurley, M., Lemen, L.C. and Heilman, K. M. (2004). Aberrant auditory processing and atypical planum temporale in developmental stuttering. *Neurology*, *63*, 1640–6.

Hernandez, M. D. (1999). Temperament at 4 years: The contributions of handedness, gender and IQ (lateralisation). *Dissertation Abstracts International: Section B: The Sciences and Engineering*, *59*(11-B), 6092. (Dissertation Abstract-1999–95010–036).

Lane, A. B., Foundas, A. L. and Leonard, C. M. (2001). The evolution of neuro-imaging research and developmental language disorders. *Topics in Language Disorders*, *21*, 20–41.

Segal, N. I. (1989). Origins and implications of handedness and relative birth weights for IQ in monozygotic twin pairs. *Neuropsychologia, 37(4)*, 349–61.

Star signs

Fuzeau-Braesch, S. (1998). Are personality differences between twins predicted by astrology? Comment. *Personality and Individual Differences, 21(3)*, 455–7.

Television

From the available research, there is no evidence that the amount of television viewing affects IQ.

Gortmaker, S. L., Salter, C. A., Walker, D. K. (1990). The impact of television viewing on mental aptitude and achievement: A longitudinal study. *Public Opinion Quarterly, 54(4)*, 594–604.

Rural–urban differences

About 50 years ago, average rural–urban IQ differences were substantial, but they have now reduced to nothing. This is primarily due to the increasing similarity in experiences between rural and urban dwellers, the improvements in schooling capacity of both rural and urban schools and the increasing sophistication of farming practices.

Glossary

Bias   a term used to denote whether certain groups of people have an advantage of getting an item correct compared with other groups of test-takers. Bias is typically related to an item having more than one underlying dimension, usually a secondary, unintended one such as a mathematical question (primary dimension) with a rugby context (secondary dimension). Mathematical ability alone should be the reason people get the question correct and not their knowledge of rugby. In this example it might be that males have an added advantage of getting the item correct as they may have more knowledge of rugby, thus the item is biased in favour of males.

Correlation   a statistic for measuring the strength and direction of the relationship between two variables measured on the same person. For example, a correlation of .80 between achievement test scores and the amount of books in the home would suggest that people with high scores on achievement tests tend to have more books at home. Correlations range between −1.00 and 1.00, with 0.00 indicating no relationship between scores on two variables.

Cronbach's alpha   a statistic to quantify the consistency among the items in measuring a person's true score. It can be thought of as the average of the inter-item correlations. The higher the reliability ($>.70$) the more confident you can be that the items are consistently measuring a person's true score.

Effect-size	a statistical value that summarises the relationship between two variables within a statistical population. An effect-size can also be used to quantify differences between groups.
Factor analysis	a statistical method used to reduce large amounts of data into meaningful clusters. For example, questions written to measure mathematical ability and questions measuring motivations should correlate more highly among each other. So, the mathematics questions should all be correlated more highly with each other but not with the motivation questions, and vice versa.
Factor loading	the degree to which a question is related to the underlying factor: the higher the number, the stronger the relationship between the item and the factor.
Gold standard	a criterion measure. Typically the test being developed is correlated to the criterion or 'gold standard' test.
Intelligence quotient	a number that quantifies a person's intelligence.
Item difficulty	is related to the amount of people who get the item correct in relation to all those who take the item. Thus, if 100 people attempt the item and 80 people get it correct then it is an easy item $(80/100 = .80)$
Item discrimination	relates an individual's performance on an item to their overall test score. People with a higher ability should get difficult items correct and do well on the overall test. People with a lower ability should get more difficult items wrong and do less well on the test.
Item distractors	a four-choice item will have one correct answer (the keyed correct one) and three distractor answers. The idea of the distractors is that they should be equally plausible to those who are not at the ability level needed to attain the correct answer.
Item information	is related to the error associated with each item. An item with low error has higher information that is analogous to how accurately the item measures that it is measuring

at a certain level of difficulty. In other words, items with high amounts of information have great precision in estimating a person's ability at a particular point of difficulty.

Item response theory	a mathematical model that relates an individual's ability to item responses.
Item stem	the actual question statement.
Items	the questions in a test.
Normal distribution	a bell-shaped curve representing the distribution of a set of scores that are clustered around an average score.
Norms	a comparison score in relation to other test-takers scores.
Percentile	a value on a variable where a percentage of the scores fall. For example, if someone had a score at the seventy-fifth percentile, then this is the point where 75 per cent test-takers score below.
Psychological constructs	unobservable psychological entities such as confidence, self-esteem and motivation, etc.
Psychometrics	a branch of applied statistics that studies the theory and measurement of psychological attributes such as confidence, self-esteem and motivation, etc.
Reliability	a theory relating to the consistent measurement of a person's 'true' score.
Standard deviation	is a measure of variability in a distribution of scores. The higher the standard deviation, the greater the spread of scores in the distribution from the mean score.
Test information function	the sum of the item information function curves. With large amounts of items, tests can be constructed to provide maximum precision (low error) of ability at any chosen degree of difficulty for a test. Simply select items that have high information around the point of difficulty.

Unidimensionality   an assumption that an item or a set of items measure only one psychological construct – for example, verbal ability or spatial reasoning.

Validity   the appropriateness of evidence to defend the interpretations and actions derived from tests.

Variable   an entity that can take on different numerical values – for example, height, weight, IQ, etc.

References

Ackerman, P. L. (1996). A theory of adult intellectual development, process, personality, interests and knowledge. *Intelligence, 22*, 227–57.

Akbari, R. and Hosseini, K. (2008). Multiple intelligences and language learning strategies: Investigating possible relations. *System, 36*, 141–55.

Baltes, P. B. and Baltes, M. M. (1990). Psychological perspectives on successful aging: The model of selective optimisation with compensation. In P. B. Baltes and M. M. Baltes (eds), *Successful Aging: Perspectives from the Behavioural Science* (pp. 1–34). New York: Cambridge University Press.

Biggs J. B. (1996). Paradoxes of the Chinese learner. In D. Watkins and J. Biggs (eds), *The Chinese Learner: Research and Practice.* Hong Kong: Centre for Comparative Research in Education / Camberwell, Vic.: Australian Council for Educational Research.

Binet, S. (1916). *The development of intelligence in children.* Baltimore, MD: Williams & Wilkins.

Bodanis, D. (2000). *E=MC²: A Biography of the World's most Famous Equation.* New York: Berkeley Books.

Bonnet, M. H. and Arand, D. L. (2001). Impact of activity and arousal upon spectral EEG parameters. *Physiology & Behavior, 74*, 291–8

Boring, E. G. (1923). Intelligence as the tests test it. *New Republic* (6 June), 35–7.

Carroll, J. B. (1993). *Human Cognitive Abilities: A Survey of Factor-Analytical Studies.* New York: Cambridge University Press.

Cattell, R. B. (1971). *Abilities: Their Structure, Growth, and Action.* New York: Houghton Mifflin.

Ceci, S. J. (1991). How much does schooling influence general intelligence and its cognitive components? A reassessment of the evidence. *Developmental Psychology, 37*, 703–22.

Ceci, S. J. (1996). *On Intelligence: A Bioecological Treatise on Intellectual Development.* Cambridge, MA: Harvard University Press.

Ceci, S. J. (2003). Cast in six ponds and you'll reel in something: Looking back on 25 years of research. *American Psychologist,* (November) 855–64.

Cohen, J. (1969) *Statistical Power Analysis for the Behavioral Sciences.* New York: Academic Press.

Corballis, M. C. and Beale, I. L. (1993). Orton revisited: Dyslexia, laterality, and left–right confusion. In D. M. Willows, R. S. Kruk and E. Corcos (eds), *Visual Processes in Reading and Reading Disabilities* (pp. 57–73). Hillsdale, NJ: Lawrence Erlbaum.

Corballis, M. C., Hattie, J. and Fletcher, R. (2008). Handedness and intellectual achievement: An even-handed look. *Neuropsychologia, 46,* 374–8.

Cornford, F. M. (1935). *Plato's Theory of Knowledge: The Theaetetus and the Sophist of Plato.* Trans. F. M. Cornford. London: Routledge.

Dweck, C. S. (1999) *Self-theories: Their Role in Motivation, Personality, and Development.* Hove: Psychology Press, Taylor & Francis Group.

Fletcher, R. J. and Hattie, J. A. C. (2004). Test the Nation: The development of an IQ test for New Zealand adults – 2004. *Psychological Reports, 102(2),* 389–97.

Flynn, J. R. (1987). Massive IQ gains in 14 nations: What IQ tests really measure. *Psychological Bulletin, 101,* 171–91.

Flynn, J. R. (2007). *What is Intelligence? Beyond the Flynn Effect.* Cambridge: Cambridge University Press.

Foundas, A. L., Bollich, A. M., Feldman, J., Corey, D. M., Hurley, M., Lerman, L. C., Heilman, K. M. (2004). Aberrant auditory processing and atypical planum temporale in Developmental Stuttering. *Neurology, 61,* 1640–6.

Galton, F. (1869). *Hereditary Genius.* London: MacMillan.

Galton, F. (1907). *Inquiries into Human Faculty and its Development* (2nd edn). London: J. M. Dent & Co.

Gardner, H. (1983) *Frames of Mind: The Theory of Multiple Intelligences.* New York: Basic Books.

Gardner, H. (1999) *Intelligence Reframed: Multiple Intelligences for the 21st Century.* New York: Basic Books.

Goldstein, D., Hahn, C. S., Hasher, L., Wiprzycka, U. and Zelazo, P. D. (2007). Time of day, intellectual performance, and behavioral problems in morning versus evening type adolescents: Is there a synchrony effect? *Personality and Individual Differences, 42(3),* 431–40

Gottfredson, L. S. (1997). Mainstream science on intelligence: An editorial with 52 signatories, history, and bibliography. *Intelligence, 24,* 13–23.

Gould, S. J. (1981). *The Mismeasure of Man.* New York: W. W. Norton and Co.

Guilford, J. P. (1967). *The Nature of Intelligence*. New York: McGraw-Hill.

Gustafsson, J. (1984). A unifying model of the structure of intellectual abilities. *Intelligence, 8,* 179–203.

Hattie, J. A. (1987). Patterns of usage and some psychometric properties of the Stanford–Binet Intelligence test. *Australian Journal of Psychology, 23,* 1–11.

Hattie, J. A. (1991). The Burt controversy: An essay review of Hearnshaw's and Joynson's biographies of Sir Cyril Burt. *Alberta Journal of Educational Research, 37,* 259–75.

Hattie, J. A. (2009). *Visible Learning: A Synthesis of 800+ Meta-Analyses on Achievement.* Oxford: Routledge.

Hearnshaw, L. (1979). *Cyril Burt: Psychologist.* Ithaca, NY: Cornell University Press.

Herrnstein, R. and Murray, C. (1994) *The Bell Curve: Intelligence and Class Structure in American Life.* New York: Free Press.

Horn, J. L. and Cattell, R. B. (1966). Refinement and test of the theory of fluid and crystallized intelligence. *Journal of Educational Psychology, 57(5),* 253–70.

Howe, M. J. A. (1997). *IQ in Question: The Truth About Intelligence.* London: Sage.

Hunt, T. (1928). The measurement of social intelligence. *Journal of Applied Psychology, 12,* 317–34.

Jencks, C. (1972). *Inequality: A Reassessment of the Effect of Family and Schooling in America.* New York: Harper & Row.

Jensen, A. R. (1969). How much can we boost I.Q. and scholastic achievement? *Harvard Educational Review, 33,* 1–123.

Jensen, A. R. (1998). *The g Factor: The Science of Mental Ability.* Westport, CT: Praeger.

Joynson, R. B. (1989). *The Burt Affair.* New York: Routledge.

Karabel, J. (2005). *The Chosen.* Boston, MA: Houghton Mifflin.

Lane, A. B., Foundas, A. L. and Leonard, C. M. (2001). The evolution of neuro-imaging research and developmental language disorders. *Topics in Language Disorders, 21,* 20–41.

Lynn, R. and Vanhanen, T. (2002). *IQ and the Wealth of Nations.* Westport, CT: Praeger.

Neisser, U. (1977). Rising scores on intelligence tests. *American Scientist* **85:** 440–7 (September/October).

Orton, S. T. (1937). *Reading, Writing, and Speech Problems in Children.* New York: W. W. Norton & Co.

Penrose, L. S. and Raven, J. C. (1936). A new series of perceptual tests: A preliminary communication. *British Journal of Medical Psychology, 16,* 97–104.

Roberts, R. D., Stankov, L., Schulze, R. and Kyllonen, P. C. (2008). Extending intelligence: Conclusions and future directions. In P. C. Kyllonen, R. D. Roberts, L. Stankov (eds), *Extending Intelligence* (pp. 363–78). Malwah, NJ: Lawrence Erlbaum.

Roenneberg, T., Wirz-Justice, A. and Merrow, M. (2003). Life between clocks – daily temporal patterns of human chronotypes. *Journal of Biological Rhythms*, *18*, 80–90.

Schmidt, F. and Hunter, J. (2004). General mental ability in the world of work: Occupational attainment and job performance. *Journal of Personality and Social Psychology*, *86(1)*, 162–73.

Spearman, C. (1904). General intelligence objectively determined and measured. *American Journal of Psychology*, *15*, 201–93.

Sternberg, R. J. (1985a). Implicit theories of intelligence, creativity, and wisdom. *Journal of Personality and Social Psychology*, *49*, 607–27.

Sternberg, R. J. (1985b). *Beyond IQ: A Triarchic Theory of Intelligence*. Cambridge: Cambridge University Press.

Sternberg, R. J. and Detterman, D. K. (eds) (1986). *What is Intelligence? Contemporary Viewpoints on its Nature and Definition*. Norwood, NJ: Ablex.

Thorndike, E. (1921). *The Teacher's Word Book*. New York: Teachers College.

Thurstone, L. L. (1938). *Primary Mental Abilities*. Chicago: University of Chicago Press.

Wainer, H. and Robinson, D. H. (2009). Profiles in research: Linda S. Gottfredson. *Journal of Educational and Behavioral Statistics*, *34(3)*, 395–427.

Wechsler, D. (1939). *The Measurement of Adult Intelligence*. Baltimore: Williams & Wilkins.

Wechsler, D. (1975). Intelligence defined and undefined: A relativistic appraisal. *American Psychologist*, *30*, 135–9.

Wechsler, D. (1997). *Wechsler Adult Intelligence Scale* (3rd edn). San Antonio, TX: The Psychological Corporation.

Wechsler, D. (2008). *Wechsler Adult Intelligence Scale* (4th edn). San Antonio, TX: The Psychological Corporation.

Witelson, S. F., Kigar, D. L. and Harvey, T. (1999). The exceptional brain of Albert Einstein. *Lancet*, *353*, 2149–53.

Wittgenstein, L. (1958). *Philosophical Investigations* (2nd edn). Trans. G. E. M. Anscombe. Oxford: Blackwell.

Zenderland, L. (1998). *Measuring Minds: Henry Herbert Goddard and the Origins of American Intelligence Testing*. Cambridge: Cambridge University Press.

Index

www.routledge.com/education

2nd Edition

The Psychology of Education

Martyn Long, Educational Psychologist, UK
Clare Wood, University of Coventry, UK
Karen Littleton,The Open University, UK
Terri Passenger, Nuffield Hospital Cheltenham, UK
Kieron Sheehy, The Open University, UK

Written in an accessible and engaging style, this second edition of *The Psychology of Education* addresses key concepts from psychology which relate to education. Throughout the text the author team emphasise an evidence-based approach, providing practical suggestions to improve learning outcomes, while fictional case studies are used in this new edition to provide students with a sense of what psychological issues can look like in the classroom. Activities around these case studies give students the chance to think about how to apply their theoretical knowledge to these real-world contexts.

A chapter on learning interactions and social worlds is new to this edition. The following chapters have all been extensively updated:

- Learning
- Assessment
- Individual differences and achievement
- Student engagement and motivation
- The educational context
- Society and culture
- Language
- Literacy
- Inclusive education and special educational needs
- Behaviour problems
- Dealing with behaviour problems.

This book is essential reading for undergraduate students of Education Studies and Psychology as well as trainee teachers on BA, BEd and PGCE courses. It will also be of use to postgraduates training to be educational psychologists.

November 2010: 448pp
Hb: 978-0-415-48689-7:
£75.00
Pb: 978-0-415-48690-3:
£24.99
eBook: 978-0-203-84009-2

For more information and to order a copy visit
www.routledge.com/9780415486903

Available from all good bookshops

Contemporary Theories of Learning

Learning Theorists ... In Their Own Words

Edited by **Knud Illeris**, Danish University of Education, Denmark

In this definitive collection of today's most influential learning theorists, sixteen world-renowned experts present their understanding of what learning is and how human learning takes place.

Professor Knud Illeris has collected chapters that explain both the complex frameworks in which learning takes place and the specific facets of learning, such as the acquisition of learning content, personal development, and the cultural and social nature of learning processes. Each international expert provides either a seminal text or an entirely new précis of the conceptual framework they have developed over a lifetime of study.

Elucidating the key concepts of learning, *Contemporary Theories of Learning* provides both the perfect desk reference and an ideal introduction for students. It will prove an authoritative guide for researchers and academics involved in the study of learning, and an invaluable resource for all those dealing with learning in daily life and work. It provides a detailed synthesis of current learning theories... all in the words of the theorists themselves.

December 2008: 256pp
Hb: 978-0-415-47343-9:
£85.00
Pb: 978-0-415-47344-6:
£21.99
eBook: 978-0-203-87042-6